BOOK TESTIMONIALS

I enjoy business leadership articles, biographies and marine history so a book that combined all three is worth a read. The juxtaposition between the primitive technology, catastrophic risk, and social order versus modern knowledge of leadership makes this book a worthwhile read.

The authors draw out principles and tenets of leadership and skillfully refines them into modern leadership lessons. The self-assessments at the end of each chapter are useful to help a leader put the principles into action. Overall, the authors validate that principled leadership is ageless.

Mark Easden
Chief Operating Officer
Dale & Lessmann LLP

Cox and Warn have written a remarkable book.
Using the real life epic journey of explorer Shackleton, as a skeleton, they have fleshed out the form to show numerous instances and examples of leadership principles in action.

The authors ask us to join them as they follow Shackleton, through his horrific life threatening journey, and take advantage of each setback to illustrate Shackleton's inherent genius at leadership.

From the earliest revelation that "the map is not the territory", they use the explorer's actions to demonstrate the author's "Seven Cs" of leadership.
It is a fantastic journey which continually challenges the reader to self assess his perception of leadership.

John R. Vickers P. Eng.
Past President Canadian Foundry Association,
Past President Royal Hamilton Yacht Club
Past C.E. O. Westinghouse Air Bake Casting Division.

Your dedication page was enough for me to get started, everybody has a place and needs an opportunity. In my early twenties I found myself in a middle management role and over the years I intuitively found ways to manage. A book like this would have been such a great help!

A leader who does not walk the talk soon loses the moral authority to lead others...
I love the quote: " Once we commit, providence moves in." Goethe. Leaders must take action, commit and be prepared to handle what comes next...
I look forward to seeing this book published as it will have a place to help leaders in family, business and organizations.

Len Verhey
President, Canway Equipment Manufacturing Inc.

The authors skillfully and richly illustrate how to move from the leadership approach of managing numbers and cutting people to creating wins for leaders, followers, communities, and the world.

You will want to read this book twice and refer to it regularly. The authors provide the responsible leader with depth of insight and much encouragement, richly supported by quotes from numerous acknowledged world leaders throughout history.

The authors have clearly lived what they write. This book will be inspiring for the responsible leader who rejects the notion of self-focussed leadership.

"Tectonic forces that are shifting and reshaping our world"... make this book an imperative for modern, altruistic leaders.

There is toxic leadership, and there is responsible leadership. The authors skillfully help the aspiring leader towards the latter.

This book provides hope for humanity.

Iain P. Murray, PhD
Professor Emeritus
Gordon S. Lang School of Business and Economics
University of Guelph

We all love a good story. The authors take us on a journey exploring leadership in contemporary, challenging, and crisis contexts by using illustrative narrative and illuminating paintings from the story of Sir Shackleton's Antarctica expedition. This book charts territory applicable for leadership lessons today.

Cynthia Cherrey, PhD, | President and CEO
International Leadership Association
Moller Institute Leadership Fellow, Cambridge University

Copyright © 2019 Dr. Michael Cox and Dr. James Warn.
All rights reserved.
ISBN 9781725685659

To order additional copies visit Amazon.com
To learn about the authors, visit their sites on Linkedin.com

DEDICATION

This book is dedicated to responsible principled leaders
Those who live by an ethos that embraces hope, resilience, courage and
meaningful opportunity for others to also serve and lead.

Fortitudine Vincimus
"By Endurance, We Conquer."

Shackleton.

ACKNOWLEDGEMENTS

This book is the result of extensive international field research in the practice of principled leadership in contemporary, challenging and crisis contexts. This included field research in the U.S., Canada, U.K., Australia, New Zealand, Netherlands and China. The work involved extensive dialogue with leading faculty, thought leaders and practitioners in the field of leadership in both public and private sectors. The nexus of research, teaching and strategic leadership in the field, hostile conditions and the classroom created a rigorous leadership development environment. This involved the testing of principles and approaches and the mentoring of career professionals from diverse organizations engaged in leadership programs at the University of Guelph and University of New South Wales at Australian Defence Force Academy. It required experiencing first-hand frozen terrain, rough seas and desert conditions to learn how the mind of the leader can overcome conditions to lead and excel. A special acknowledgement is in recognition of the leaders in the field and the career professionals in the leadership programs. These talented individuals strengthened the dialogue in advancing the leadership thinking, principles and practice in demanding contexts. This included many exceptional men and women from all levels of organization. The opinion leaders at the edge of leadership include:

Dr. Brian Earn, The Tuck School of Leadership, Dartmouth College. Dr. Cynthia Cherrey, President, International Leadership Association. Denys Amyot, Former President, Canadian School of Public Service. Dr. Xu Gai, Research Dept., China Executive Leadership Academy, Pudong. Lieutenant General, Michel Maisonneuve, former chief of staff NATO supreme allied command. Dr. Ian Macdonald, Director, Public Administration Program, Schulich School of Business. Dr. Anders Hytter, Department of Leadership, Vaxjo University, Sweden. Dr. Alistair McIntyre, Faculty, Defence Research Academy. Dr. Jack Muscat, Leadership Psychologist. Staff Superintendent Darren Smith, Toronto Police College. Professor John Gosling, Former Director

Centre for Leadership, University of Exeter. Dr John Walsh, Vice Provost, University of Guelph-Humber. Dr. Joe Barth, Professor Emeritus, MBA Graduate Faculty, Professor Erna Van Duren, Strategic Management Case Leadership Faculty ad Professor Emeritus, Jim Pickworth, University of Guelph. Dr. Alan Okros, former Director, The Canadian Forces Leadership Institute. Dr. Sylvain Charlebois, Dean, School of Business, Dalhousie University. Lieutenant Colonel Colin Magee, PhD on his work on collaborative leadership and Dr. Iain Murray, graduate faculty and former serving officer, as we endured many winter hiking and trekking sessions in minus twenty-degree weather conditions to experience and appreciate frozen contexts. Brigadier Nick Jans, Australian Defense Force and the many talented career professional graduates from defense, police, EMS, health care and the serving professions in public and private sector that we have had the privilege to work with on complex issues and applied research to build leadership capability. This includes those exceptional and dedicated individuals who are in the serving professions and have completed leadership programs and applied research to advance their leadership capability. Many of their names are not published here for security reasons. They served on operations in Afghanistan, Bosnia, as front-line police officers, Fire Service officers, Health care professionals, service, sports leadership and hospitality professionals.

To all the men and women who we have worked with in advancing leadership in these organizations, we are deeply grateful. To ensure the leadership practice has impact and relevance it was decided to integrate a real-life story of principled leadership in a challenging context. The authors selected an exemplar of leadership Ernest Shackleton, the intrepid Antarctic explorer. This was tested working with teams from the serving professions using real life case study examples of Shackleton's leadership and his crew in the Antarctic. The results were resounding from participants in how this brought leadership alive and made the principles and practices highly relevant to their own context. The authors conducted further research to ensure the leadership narrative has depth and rigour. This included visits to the

National Maritime Museum, Greenwich, London. Among the collections is the actual boat, the James Caird, that was used for Shackleton's open sea rescue. At Cambridge University there is a Shackleton Archive and a collection of artefacts and letters of correspondence. The authors spent time at the Royal Naval and Australian Maritime Museums to attain understanding of the lives of the intrepid leaders and crews working in complex contexts.

Appreciation to The Royal Hamilton Yacht Club a community–driven sail-training organization that embody the Corinthian spirit. In this distinct culture the 7Cs as a shared narrative is woven into both success and survival. Facilitation of leadership development on locale addressed responsible leadership principles for future young leader's to engender the spirit to serve, lead and excel.

Finally, gratitude and respect to the late Thomas Frederick Cox, 42 Commando, Royal Marines. His fatherly leadership in words and deeds from earlier days continue to speak to one of the authors of the importance of mind over matter and self-determination for personal resilience to serve, lead and support others.

To our family and friends our thanks and appreciation in being part of this long-distance endurance leadership journey.

Leadership Challenges From the Edge of Experience

*Shackleton's Leadership Principles
To Serve, Lead and Excel.*

Dr. Michael Cox, PhD CD
Professor Emeritus and Former Director
Centre for Studies in Leadership, University of Guelph

Dr. James Warn, PhD MAPS
Former Head School of Business and Leadership Programs
University of New South Wales Canberra at
Australian Defence Force Academy

Leadership Challenges
From the Edge of Experience

Shackleton's Trusted Leadership Principles
To Serve, Lead and Excel in Changing Contexts.

TABLE OF CONTENTS

	Page
Acknowledgements	vii
Table of Contents	3
Preface	4
Introduction: Leadership Challenges and Principles	9
Chapter 1: Leadership Context	19
Chapter 2: Leadership Consciousness	39
Chapter 3: Leadership Character	59
Chapter 4: Leadership Confidence	83
Chapter 5: Leadership Courage	95
Chapter 6: Leadership Commitment	111
Chapter 7: Leadership Capability	127
Chapter 8: Responsible Leadership in Action	137
Responsible Leadership Log	152
General References and Selected Bibliography	155
Authors' Relevant Publications	159
Author's Profile	162

PREFACE

Many books on leadership have been written that focus on a narrow prism around a corporate leadership narrative based on short-term thinking and narrow metrics. This book is different. It explores the timeless challenges that leaders face in order to derive principles around which it is possible to develop responsible and effective leadership practices. This book uses a real-life narrative of leadership on the edge of experience to explain what matters for oneself to develop mastery in principled leadership to fully inform character, competence and capability. We challenge the reader by linking theory, applied research and practice using a real-life narrative of Sir Ernest Shackleton the Antarctic explorer, who despite all odds, maintained his team in the face of adversity and led them to safety. This is a gripping true story of leadership and survival. This narrative offers examples that are pertinent to everyday leadership practice in our current time and demonstrates a leadership ethos to serve, lead and excel.

Ernest Shackleton was an Antarctic expedition leader attempting to push the boundaries of what was humanly possible to extend our scientific understanding of the South Pole. Shackleton led three trips to Antarctica and is best known for keeping his team together, dedicated to the task and focused under the most adverse, disastrous and hostile conditions. His leadership role was truly heroic.

Being a leader is different to being a manager. Leaders operate in a world of uncertainty, ambiguity and change. On the other hand, managers administer organisational systems and mange people and resources under predicted and understood circumstances. Leaders, however, operate on the edge of experience. Leadership is future oriented and requires new thinking and skills to adapt in an undefined and sometimes unformed territory.

There are certain timeless dynamics to being a leader and influencing others to achieve outcomes. Regardless of whether you are a leader in a senior organisational role with all the authority power that position entails, or a young activist attempting to mobilize people around a cause, the challenges faced are much the same. We have used the metaphor of the Seven Seas (7Cs), the edge of experience, to frame these challenges: Context, Consciousness, Character, Confidence, Courage, Commitment and Capability. By analyzing these challenges within the narrative of a real-life leadership experience we identify leadership principles.

Embedding these principles with a real-life narrative enables us to respect the complexity of leadership, its uncertainty, and untidiness. Even though Shackleton achieved a remarkable outcome with his team, he was still human and cannot be idolized as a perfect leader. What is remarkable is that an imperfect person can rise to the occasion and overcame elemental leadership challenges. This book provides a framework of principles that will offer you a pathway for your own applied learning as a resilient responsible leader. At times the learning will be inspirational, and the aim of the book is to unlock your capacity to succeed and lead effectively in a contemporary, globalized workplace and society that often presents diverse and contrary contexts.

The book integrates leadership principles to inform a state of mind that respects current applied research on leadership and resilience. Our approach advances leadership from its comfort zone by creating a real-life context to develop a deep perspective for making sense of leadership in the world now. This book combines lifetime bodies of work of the two authors who are internationally respected professors in the field of leadership, strategy and psychology. Both are practitioners of leadership and have mentored high-potential professionals in leading organizations and worked with and learned of their challenges.

Dr Cox and Dr Warn are both former serving officers with the Canadian and Australian Defense Forces, respectively. We have developed leadership programs for the private, public and volunteer sectors and have prepared professionals to succeed in defense, police, emergency service, health, education, financial, hospitality, food, service and NGO sectors. As a result, considerable knowledge transfers have validated emergent leadership approaches in complex and crisis contexts. Their experience in these leadership contexts has convinced us of the need for a responsible leadership ethos founded on principles to sustain individual resilience and capability. The authors have worked for over a decade in a collaboration to field test the principles in a range of contexts. We believe we have developed a considered understanding of emergent approaches for individuals and organizations with distinct professional identities, culture and inter-organizational challenges.

Developing Responsible Leadership in Words, Deeds and Actions.

These insights are unlocked for the first time in one book that integrates seven trusted principles as a pathway for exemplary leadership. The principled process is explained for individuals to identify ways to leverage capability and build resilience in a context of change. This book has been written so that lessons derived from real experience can be applied in daily practice. Understanding how these challenges manifest in your own leadership practice will help identify "say-do" gaps to self-master a state of mind, and a positive spirit to serve, lead and excel.

To benefit from the applied learning, it is worth developing your own record of self-reflection, and to kick start the process we have included a *Leadership Log* at the end of each chapter. This mental discipline will enable you to recognize better your own individual leadership challenges and regular self-reflection will trigger the insights into shaping yourself as a responsible leader.

Each chapter explores facets of the Shackleton narrative that provide opportunity to deepen our understanding of the state of mind needed to lead in diverse contexts. As we studied the detail of Shackleton's expedition, we became more and more impressed with his leadership and its applicability to our contemporary leadership challenges. At a superficial level, the Shackleton story is a tale of derring-do. Studying these actual events, however, we came to realize that it is a well-documented experience of a leader being able to pull together a diverse and headstrong group of individuals to get them to work together as a team and overcome impending disaster. Michael Cox was so inspired by the Shackleton experience that he painted a series of paintings around key events and has illustrated each chapter with one of them. We hope that you too will be inspired by the Shackleton experience and the paintings will help you to visualize and bring alive the unfolding leadership narrative.

Think of the book as embarking on a leadership journey. Be prepared to step out of your comfort zone to perform in an environment where you cannot give up and you must develop resources to shape the outcome. Be prepared to know yourself in a challenging leadership context. We hope you enjoy this journey of self-discovery to be a better leader.

Michael Cox PhD CD

James Warn PhD MAPS

INTRODUCTION

Leadership Challenges from the Edge of Experience
Shackleton's Trusted Leadership Principles
To Serve, Lead and Excel.

This leadership story you are about to read sounds impossible. It is also inspiring, insightful and true.

Shackleton's narrative of this incredible polar voyage highlights leadership challenges that are enduring and universal and relevant to leaders today. In following the epic journey of Shackleton and his team we can derive principles and demonstrate how they work in real life to inspire leadership and followership to serve, lead and excel.

You may not have considered Antarctica or any Polar region as a context to study leadership in practice, but this book gives a new perspective on exemplary leadership.

Through it, it will help you to make sense of leading and being resilient and successful in an age of disruption, fluidity, rapid changes and transformation.

The true story of the exemplary leadership of Sir Ernest Shackleton reformulates our understanding of leadership theory, research and practice. We distil lessons learned from Shackleton's incredible story of leadership, followership, courage and survival and group these lessons under the metaphor of "the Seven Seas" (our metaphor for the 7 challenges of leadership).

You might wonder why we decided to use the Seven Seas (7Cs) metaphor. Well, for the people of ancient Greece the Seven Seas referred to the known bodies of water around the Mediterranean along which trade and exploration were conducted. However, as explorers pushed the boundaries of human experience, the exact nature of the seas changed. Different historical periods opened up new sets of seas and in contemporary times the seven seas refer to the major oceans of the earth.

We are using the metaphor of "the Seven Seas" in reference to living leadership in new and challenging spaces. And, we are looking to times of leadership when you are on the edge of experience and conception of the known world. In this book we ask you to join us in exploring the seven challenges of leadership (the 7Cs). The seven seas we navigate in this book are: Context, Consciousness, Character, Confidence, Courage, Commitment and Capability. As we navigate these seven challenges (the 7Cs) we can frame the leadership qualities exemplified by Shackleton in an amazing journal of survival and hope undertaken to save his crew after the Antarctic ice had destroyed their ship.

Leadership is most valued when it occurs on the borderline of our understanding and grasp of the changing world. Throughout the book we draw on the experience of Sir Ernest Shackleton who led an expedition to the Antarctic, which literally in that historical era, was the end of the earth. Shackleton tackled numerous challenges as a leader, and importantly had to adapt his leadership focus in the face of unexpected setbacks and an unrelentingly hostile and unforgiving environment. The experience of Shackleton highlights the impact a leader can make when they apply the skills of a wholly-rounded person in working with a team. In organisations, the importance of this well-rounded development of the individual leader is often overlooked as management becomes focused on metrics and meeting deadlines. Also, other participants in the leadership industry, namely business schools and consultants seek to support the management hierarchy and focus on easy to remember sets of skills rather than engaging in the hard work of developing individuals as responsible leaders. This book takes a different perspective. We do not put forward any easy answers or list of leadership attributes. Instead we invite you to explore real life leadership challenges to embark on your own journey to the Seven Seas of self-discovery and insight.

Leadership to serve and lead others in any context is founded on a healthy mind, body and spirit.

A holistic understanding of the leader is vital for achieving outcomes in complex situations. In this book we explore the meaning of exemplary leadership. Self-development at a holistic level is an outcome of lifelong growth and advancement that is focused on the principle of "to serve and to excel". To achieve transformational change requires a willingness to learn from experience, to self-reflect and to be guided by key values. A diligent approach to self-development will require fostering in yourself a leadership mindset that perceives the world through the prism of what we call "super intelligence" – which is the integration of ethos (social intelligence), pathos (emotional intelligence) and logos (truthfulness).

Trusted Principles to live, lead, serve and excel in any context.

"Super intelligence" endows the leader with a moral prism to understand and implement principled leadership decisions in contexts based on an informed perspective. The *"7Cs of Leadership"* offers a framework to recognize, develop and maintain individual strengths and limitations for self-mastery and self-development as a leader. In this applied learning process, we integrate research and theory to state the lessons learnt as a set of seven trusted principles. These principles are anchored in our experiences in mentoring in leadership programs for career professionals and in complex work contexts.

In the contemporary world context, we are challenged by the tectonic forces that are shifting and reshaping our understanding of leadership practice, organization arrangements and socio-political norms. Countervailing values and relentless waves of information, intelligent algorithms that second-guess our behavior, artificial intelligence, networked technology, superior surveillance and security breaches all pitch our world view into turmoil and cause an erosion of trust. These are reshaping how we think, learn, plan and what we already know. The old legacy of 'organizational thinking' is shifting into 'the learning and knowing organization'. This can be stressful and perplexing.

Another condition of our times is that we are forced to live and react in the present, so we often fail to see that leaders living in the past were faced by similar crisis, chaos, confusion and conflict of a truly global nature. However, we believe you can learn to navigate and create authentic leadership paths that are trusted, principled and resilient to sustain you on the leadership journey.

We invite you to embark as a leader, captain, navigator and explorer on this authentic leadership journey across the Seven Seas (7Cs) of leadership as we establish principles to serve, lead and excel.

Be prepared to "know yourself" in making emotional, intellectual and strategic decisions that strengthen your leadership competence and capability to serve and lead with purpose today. Join us in following Shackleton and his crew on an incredible leadership journey of self-discovery that will inspire and ignite your desire and capacity to succeed and be all you can be.

Leadership habits of mind for endurance and courage to act.

The practice of leadership is ancient and in any collection of people, leaders naturally emerge, and people culturally attribute specific human traits to leadership. However, the ancient wisdom on being a leader is as relevant today as it was in earlier times. Whilst leadership in ancient and classical periods occurred in different sets of social and political organizations and institutions compared to today, the quality of the individual leader remains crucial to achieving effective followership. Ancient and classical leaders might have been tribal chiefs, kings, emperors, or heads of religious communities, but in all cases needed to influence followers and gain support, even if from a powerful few, to maintain their positions of leadership and power.

"Mens Sana in Corpore Sano" – a sound mind in a sound body.

You have probably heard of this Latin phrase "a sound mind in a sound body". It is an excerpt from a satire written by the Roman poet Juvenal in which he draws attention to the vanity of human wishes and reminds his readers that pursuing physical and mental health is the key to wellbeing. Rather than wishing for passing whims, Juvenal is saying that wellbeing depends on balancing physical and mental health in a virtuous way. This ancient insight invigorates the modern concept of what we have called super-intelligence - the balance of ethos (ethical strength), pathos (emotional intelligence) and logos (truthfulness).

'Ethos' is the social responsibility and ethical foundations of the leader, 'pathos' is the capacity to connect with others in an empathetic and humane way, and 'logos' refers to the application of appropriate thinking and reasoning to a situation. Achieving 'super intelligence' requires the leader to understand, internalize and action the seven foundational principles of leadership. Implementing these 7C principles results in a well-balanced individual able to have impact in organizations that are adapting, changing and thriving in fast changing and disruptive environments.

Organizations that lack a sound understanding of leadership principles move to imbalance and eventually a harmful, turbid and in some cases toxic climate.

An organization lacking responsible leadership balance becomes distorted and dysfunctional and can cause undue suffering. The cost of this reality can be found in disease clusters across the organization, sickness as well as loss of purpose, performance and resolve. CEOs, executives, board members and financial experts put a lot of attention into analyzing the financial health of a company, but too often fail to consider its psychological health.

There are many definitions of leadership, but at their core is a purpose-driven influence relationship between the leader and followers.

This book draws on scientific research into leadership, psychology and management, and other academic disciplines, with a theoretical framework in the background.

Our focus is on the lived experience of leadership.

We draw on psychology to tackle practical problems of leadership experience.

The starting point is to focus on the leadership capacity of the individual leader - to 'know thyself'. This ancient Greek aphorism, reputedly inscribed in the Temple of Apollo at Delphi, reminds us that knowing "thyself" underpins the assumptions behind modern scientific theory of emotional intelligence as well as the practice of authentic leadership.

'Know Thyself' is the foundation of self-mastery to lead.

'Know Thyself' is the foundation for principled leadership self-mastery. Leadership is about doing the right thing. It is as much an internal journey as an external capability. A leader who lacks self-awareness is not fully aware or ready to lead. Mastering leadership requires an honest self-assessment.

This book asks you to stop and reflect on where you are starting from and what needs to be cultivated to self-develop the responsible leadership ethos to serve, lead and to excel.

Knowing thyself is the key to being able to unlock and achieve an authentic principled leadership ethos to serve and lead others.

The Greek philosopher, Aristotle, identified the importance of ethos, pathos and logos to communicate ideas in a credible and convincing way to others. Ethos (credibility), or ethical appeal, means that the leader has an ethical strength that enables that leader to have a substantive and enduring social impact. Pathos (emotional) means that the leader is connected to others at a deep emotional level, shows genuine empathy and communicates at an important human level. Logos (thinking) means persuading through reasoning and being able to explain the facts of the matter to followers.

Thinking implies a capacity for critical thinking, that can assemble relevant facts, evaluate and form a judgment. The three elements of super-intelligence work together to form a whole that is stronger than the sum of its parts. Failure in any element impairs the overall capacity for leadership.

A leader who is unethical (e.g. corruptly seeking bribes) will distort thinking (e.g. be self-serving) and corrupt his or her emotional relationships with followers (e.g. abuse the trust of followers and use them for their convenience). It is through being in touch with one's own self that a leader can influence followers in an authentic manner and build a deeper and more meaningful relationship with them. In this way, a true reflective understanding of one's own ethos, pathos and logos serves as an anchor for the leader and becomes pivotal for responsible leadership.

Self-mastering principled leadership

We look beyond all the training, jargon and goals-driven fads to the little understood. If you have undertaken any self-development training, you might have been introduced to the Johari window. This tool was devised by two psychologists (Joseph Luft and Harrington Ingham) and displays a matrix to identify quadrants: (1) what is known to one self and others (2) what is known to one self but not others, and of somewhat more importance, (3) what is known to others but not oneself, that is our blind spots, and crucially for leadership (4) what is not known to oneself or others. It is this final quadrant, the unknown that can get us into the most trouble in demanding and stressful leadership situations. The uncertainty of complex leadership situations can evoke anxieties and fears from deep memories within ourselves.

Being willing to explore our deepest fears and anxieties is an important part of the leadership journey. Regular self-reflection on our thoughts and feelings in leadership situations will start to unlock some of these deeper anxieties. Some leaders may even experience a tumultuous crucible event which although stressful, does enable them to see and understand the bedrock of their own leadership. The Socratic perspective states that "the unexamined life is not worth living". This saying draws attention to the need to reflect on our fundamental values and understand how they are integrated into how we behave as a leader. Socrates understood leadership as a moral activity, and it is important to understand how our own leadership practice serves to create the moral ground for human endeavor and activity.

Leadership entails the exercise of power but also requires humility and that the leader understands followers in the pursuit of shared goals. Leaders without this grounding will find themselves in the service of narrow ideas or causes and will use power selfishly. They will no longer be nourished by inclusive values, critical dialogue or a shared process at its center, leadership dries up and becomes the wielding of power on behalf of narrow ideals.

In the past, unethical leaders have used visions and dreams to mobilize power and the will of the people to disastrous outcomes. Understanding this helps to see the important role of dialogue and its importance to knowledge transfer within a learning organization. In dialogical interactions leaders are distinguished from their followers by having greater critical perspective.

The seven principles explored in this book create understanding of how to adapt leadership to emerging situations and challenging contexts. Shackleton's narrative of his incredible voyage is used to exemplify these principles and demonstrate how they work in real life to inspire leadership and followership to serve, lead and excel.

Many leaders work in organizational, workplace and community contexts where the territory of leadership is contained, well-known, understandable, and seemingly manageable - easy to navigate.

This is not the case of leadership in an Antarctic context, which has topography, for example, that is highly unstable with hidden fissures, and deep crevices that can take life and overwhelm in an instant. It takes a leadership state of mind in these contexts to focus on objectives and lead others who willingly follow and are prepared for serious challenges. The demanding context of Antarctic or polar exploration, while extreme, is highly relevant to leaders working in fluid, ambiguous, volatile and uncertain contexts.

The collective wisdom, teachings and applied learning in this book provide inspirational lessons learned and the strategic leadership thinking required for self-mastery of a principled leadership ethos to succeed in the contemporary context.

Think of this book as your world classroom. The seven chapters help you navigate the "Seven Seas" (7Cs) to integrate the applied learning in your life to self-master the thinking, knowledge and skills to serve, lead and excel today.

Each chapter deepens your understanding of the principles to develop insight to lead in diverse contexts. This applied learning has evolved from extensive teaching, mentoring and collaborative research in the field of leadership. In our professional lives we have provided a rigorous environment to support leaders in developing informed perspective and insight of the challenges and emerging approaches.

To place this in the context of Shackleton, imagine the reality of surviving for ten months on Antarctic pack ice after your ship has been trapped, crushed and sunk.

Survival contexts bring to the fore the relevance of the 7Cs of leadership in practice.

It is important to recognize that leadership is shaped by the context and locale of operations. The Shackleton narrative shows us how to adapt when the context changes from safety to survival. An important aspect of Shackleton's leadership is how he cultivated relationships to build collective capability by consensus-making. He had no external authority to back him up, or to support him with resources. In this sense, leadership is constructed in a specific place and time between leaders and followers. This is an emerging trend in a globalized workplace.

Each chapter illustrates the importance of one of the seven principles (7Cs) of leadership in action. Each principle is brought alive with actual lessons learned from Shackleton's leadership in challenging contexts and by best practices from extensive research in leadership institutes. Woven into the applied leadership narrative in each chapter structure is the leadership thinking for recognizing principles and the challenges and application that are applicable in the contemporary context.

Each chapter is supported by academic theory and best practices gleaned from extensive field research in the world's leading leadership institutes and on locale that are relevant to the leader to succeed in making a real difference in the contemporary leadership context.

Prepare to start the journey to self-master the seven seas of principled leadership to serve, lead and excel and make your world a better place.

Chapter 1: Leadership Context
Habits of Mind, Mental maps and Mindfulness

OLD MENTAL MAPS, NEW TERRITORY AND SHAPING THE CONTEXT TO LEAD

Shackleton's ship "Endurance" trapped in the Weddell Sea.
Painting by the author based on surviving photographic plates.

"I seemed to vow to myself that some day I would go to the region of ice and snow and go on and on till I came to one of the poles of the earth, the end of the axis upon which this great ball turns. No person who has not spent a period of life in those 'stark and sullen solitudes that sentinel the Pole' will understand fully what trees and flowers, sun-flecked turf and running streams mean to the soul of a man."
Ernest Shackleton.

THE SEVEN SEAS OF LEADERSHIP - PRINCIPLES TO SERVE AND LEAD

The seven principles enable understanding of how to develop principled responsible leadership to serve and lead in changing contexts and challenging environments.

The seven principles create understanding of how to adapt principled leadership to emerging situations and challenging contexts. Shackleton's narrative of his incredible voyage is used to exemplify these principles and demonstrate how they work in real life to inspire leadership and followership to serve, lead and excel. You may not have considered Antarctica or any Polar region as a context to study leadership in practice. This demanding context is highly relevant to leaders working in changing, ambiguous and fluid contexts where follow ship is not guaranteed due to authority structures. It takes a leadership state of mind, competence, capability and personal fortitude to focus on objectives to lead others who willingly follow.

Each of the chapters illustrates the principles of leadership as practised in a survival context by an exemplary leader named Ernest Shackleton and his twenty-seven crew members. Imagine the reality of surviving for ten months on Antarctic pack ice after your ship has been trapped, crushed and sunk. This is a turning point moment for the expedition. It had not been envisaged, but it was the new reality. Survival contexts bring to the fore the relevance of the seven principles of leadership in practice. It is important to recognize that leadership is shaped by the context and locale of operations. The Shackleton narrative illustrates how to adapt when context changes from safety to survival. In a survival context with extreme temperatures it is essential to have the right state of mind. An important aspect of Shackleton's leadership is how he cultivated relationships to build collective capability by consensus-making. He had no external authority to back him up or to support him with resources. In this sense, leadership is constructed in a specific place and time between leaders and followers. This book defines how the Seven Seas (7Cs) of Leadership which shaped Shackleton's responsible leadership principles allow one to self-master a leadership capability that is transformative and enables one to achieve exceptional outcomes in the face of change, adversity and complex contexts.

THE FIRST PRINCIPLE – UNDERSTAND THE LEADERSHIP CONTEXT

> "Roll up that map, it will not be wanted these ten years."
> - William Pitt
> (Referring to a map of Europe, on hearing the news of the Battle of Austerlitz, December 1805)

> "For me context is the key – from that comes the understanding of everything." - Kenneth Noland

> "Making mental connections is our most crucial learning tool, the essence of human intelligence; to forge links; to go beyond the given; to see patterns, relationships, context." - Marilyn Ferguson

> "We had discovered an accursed country. We had found the Home of the Blizzard." - Douglas Mawson

The lived voice of responsible leadership on context. During the period of the Afghanistan conflict the authors worked with leadership personnel on deployment. A terminology was coined in this context known as 3D + C which represented the players engaged in this complex context of operations: Defense, Diplomacy, Development, Commerce. Each of the players saw the same context through a different lens. Defense has a warfighting lens with defined objectives and desired outcomes. The understanding is that here is the problem, let's fix it. Diplomacy has a lens that views political stakeholders in the context. This lens sees the world as a tango of trade-offs. Development has a lens that focuses on helping people. Others often harshly define this as a Pollyanna worldview. Then Commerce sees the context as a place to make deals and profit from the other context. Here we see firsthand the complexity of the leadership context in a place called Afghanistan, which is a tapestry of tribal alliances and diverse languages. The lesson learnt is to understand that the map is not the territory. It is ironic that treasure and lives were lost in a historical context that has defied strangers from foreign lands.

Here the authors see firsthand three distinct leadership mindsets, ethos and approaches in one context. Defense sees the world through a war-fighting lens and needs to fix things. Diplomacy has a lens that seeks compromise and consensus to find common ground. Development has a lens that sees good in people and tries to save the world. It is like three leaders with three distinct identities, ideologies and intentions of how to solve a messy problem. The big D is Defense. It has power, budgets, resources and a hammer to get its way. Is it possible that we can step back in our context at work and have the courage to find a better way to serve, lead and excel for the common good?

Leadership occurs in context in a specific time and place and what works at one time may not work at another time or place. Leadership emerges from a dynamic interaction with followers and aspects of the context shape what is needed to inform the leader. The context refers to the circumstances that form the setting for the interaction between the leader and followers. The leader needs to form a keen understanding of the context and the ways in which followers might construe and understand the context. The leader needs to form an inner understanding (the mind map) of what is happening on the outside (the context).

Shackleton had formed an integrated understanding, a mind map, of what was happening in the outer context of the Antarctic landscape. This understanding provided him a capacity to develop the perspective to act in an ethical and fair manner for leading in survival contexts. Context is the mental map of a territory that requires deep understanding to inform with perspective for intelligent decision-making. Misreading or not fully understanding the context can result in disastrous decisions like the first and last voyage of the Titanic and the surface understanding does not inform that nine tenths of the iceberg beneath the surface will result in sinking the unsinkable. To understand the first principle, leadership context, a leader should know thyself, have a true understanding of their three-dimensional intelligence prism and moral compass to guide them in known and uncharted territory.

CHALLENGE 1 – RESPONSIBLE LEADERSHIP IN CHANGING CONTEXTS

The place where leaders and followers interact

Leadership occurs in context in a specific time and place. Leadership emerges from a dynamic interaction with followers and two aspects of the context shape what is needed to inform the leader.

The leadership context for Shackleton was a world of howling gales, interspersed with frigid weather, huge icebergs, and foaming treacherous ocean currents between the pack sea ice. Movement across the ice was fraught with danger, with the ever-present threat of falling into hidden chasms and even camping on the ice floes could end in disaster, should the ice split without warning.

The leader needs to form a keen understanding of the context of their leadership, the ways in which followers might construe and understand the context (a mental map), plus the external realities.

As leadership involves the interaction between the leader and follower in a situation, the leader needs not only to understand the physical landscape, but also how people understand and interact in that environment. Shackleton's understanding of the inner (mental map) and outer (Antarctic landscape) enabled a capacity to motivate and influence followers and to attain a moral perspective which allowed him to act in an ethical and fair manner for leading in survival contexts.

Shackleton's leadership story and principles relevant to today's leaders

The leadership context is unpredictable and once the leader acts, all sorts of unexpected things can happen. That is a truism:

"Once we commit, providence moves in."

Goethe

In his account of the expedition, entitled South, Shackleton says "I have often marveled at the thin line that divides success from failure and the sudden turn that leads from apparently certain disaster to comparative safety".

To survive and succeed the leader needs to be able to form an understanding of the context that enable adaptive leadership behavior. In behavioral geography, a mental map refers to an individual's mental representation of their spatial environment and includes perceptions, knowledge, and thoughts which enable the individual to act on that environment.

Shackleton's leadership in a survival context made him acutely aware of harsh seas, shifts, changes and the need to ensure his crew stayed focused on cohesion and survival.

Mental maps to understand Changing Territory.

A leader works in a specific context. No matter what the context, it is imperative to understand the locale of operations and surrounding territory to be able to leverage strategic capability.

A mental map is a representation of what we *think* is out there in the great beyond. A map is only as good as the knowledge and skill of the people who drew it up. Mental maps are only as good while the individual understands what is happening within the immediate environment.

We develop our mental maps with experience. Remember your first job in an organization. You might have been given a copy of the organisational chart. However, it was only from experience and getting to know the people in the organization that you realized that the chart is not the territory. The chart did not show the web of relationships, the information flows, the gatekeepers, and the nodes of influence that are not always led by formal authority. It was this mental map of relationships that you realized was important for being able to exert leadership in the organization.

Adaptive leaders understand that new environments necessitate changing our mental map of reality, and leaders have an important job in enabling followers to adapt their own mental maps. Charles Turner and Alfons Trompenaars, from the Netherlands, conducted studies of managers from seven leading nations found that managers' maps focus, to differing degrees, on the perception held of past, present and future and these mental maps impact on wealth generation. How we label a context can influence how we as a leader perceive it. This can be different from the reality.

Evidence of this can be shown in how the same map can be labeled with different names such as: the Persian Gulf, The Arabian Gulf, and The Kalheej. Each name can subtly influence how we perceive cultural meanings in the region (the word Kalheej in Arabic means simply 'the gulf', and no one owns it). Mental maps are not the territory they are interpreted for sense-making and they act as filters that shape our awareness of social, political, cultural and economic worldviews. Context has subtle implications that can impact on communications and negotiations.

Once Shackleton's Incredible Voyage to Antarctica began, he quickly understood the importance of reading the context in adapting to changing situations.

Shackleton traversed Antarctica, a frozen wilderness, where the leader is exposed in front of the group and not protected by the comfort of an office and trappings of a position of authority. It is a place where follower morale and commitment to the task can soon become exhausted and respect for leadership can quickly erode. Not only did Shackleton lead, but his crew followed because of the quality of his leadership and their trust in him to succeed.

The Shackleton experience is an astonishing story of survival and hope where all 27 crew members lived for the best part of a year on frozen pack ice. They became a team with a shared sense of mission and shared purpose to survive. This outcome was achieved by leadership that was responsible, principled and enacted daily in the smallest interactions with the followers.

Shackleton: The Expedition Leader

Ernest Shackleton was an experienced Antarctic explorer who had served on expeditions with renowned leaders before taking command of his own expedition. He had personally rounded Cape Horn several times and had learned the ropes and took orders from an early age.

At age 16 Shackleton crewed on a sailing ship to Valparaiso. He rounded Cape Horn in mid-Winter. Ever the watchful apprentice, Shackleton absorbed these early lessons of good leadership versus bad. On his earlier expeditions as a crewmember he had at times experienced failure. This only strengthened his resolve to lead his own expedition despite having little money and few sponsors.

He had a keenly developed level of consciousness, determined character and confidence in others and selected volunteers who shared his passion and purpose. His style was egalitarian and authoritative - an unusual combination in an age of authoritarianism. He achieved the impossible of leading his own expedition by hard work, political savvy, grit and determination to attract sponsors, raise the finance, purchase a specially designed polar vessel and select experienced individuals to join him to turn his ambition and vision into reality.

Shackleton was a complex character, a man of great contradictions, a romantic, practical, pragmatic and, at times, patient. A strong leader with ego he was also humble and cared foremost for the wellbeing of his crew. In an age of hierarchy and privilege, his leadership and confidence were in tune with his crew, who literally would follow him to the ends of the earth.

A Leader should turn vision into reality

Ernest was an adventurer who was keen to push the boundaries of human endurance and scientific discovery. Shackleton worked hard to arouse public interest in the expedition and to obtain financial support for it from wealthy backers as well as the Royal Geographical Society. He called it the "Imperial Trans-Antarctic Expedition" in order to appeal to the patriotic emotions of fellow-citizens. Shackleton's quest was to lead a land party that would traverse the Antarctic continent. He was a persistent self-promoter who knew how to skillfully use the media to garner support. He was an excellent storyteller and had the power to share his vision and take others with him.

Although driven to return to Antarctica, Shackleton struggled with the impending period of absence from his family as well as his sense of patriotic duty to his country in view of the looming threat of war in Europe. However, Shackleton believed deeply in his mission "I believe it is in our nature to explore, to reach out into the unknown. The only true failure... would be not to explore at all".

At the same time, he was pragmatic and understood the need for public support and sponsorship to support and sustain the expedition. He was a patriot with a sense of mission and destiny. He had a keen sense of duty and occasion and used symbolism to great effect and touched an emotional chord in his fellow countrymen. King George V presented him the flag to be raised at the Pole and Queen Alexandria entrusted him with the Bible to take on the journey and wished him success.

Shackelton was flooded with over 5,000 applications from members of the public seeking to be selected as members of the expedition. One application of interest revealed the changing roles of women at the time:

> 44 Kensington Gds Sq
> Hyde park
> January 11th, 1914
>
> Dear Sir Ernest,
> We 'three sporty girls' have decided to write and beg of

you to take us with you on your expedition to the South Pole.

We are three strong, healthy girls and also gay and bright, and willing to undergo any hardships that you yourselves undergo.

If our feminine garb is inconvenient, we should just love to don masculine attire. We have been reading all books and articles that have been written on dangerous expeditions by brave men to the Polar-regions, and we do not see why men should have all the glory, and women none, especially when there are women just as brave and capable as there are men.

Trusting you will think over our suggestion,

We are Peggy Pegrine Valerie Davey and Betty Webster

P.S. We have not given any further particulars, in case you should not have time to read this, but if you are at all interested, we will write and tell you more about are greatest wish.

Shackleton politely declined their application in writing. In that era mixed sex crew were not the norm and the social norms were not developed to manage men and women living in close proximity in the crowded quarters of ships.

The members of the Expedition

Shackleton recruited an all-volunteer crew. Each team member had special skills, talents and experience. This resulted in an exceptional and diverse crew. Broadly speaking, Shackleton selected applicants to work in the following key areas: ship's crew, scientists, and explorers to traverse The Antarctic. Shackleton had a keen eye to select individuals who had resilience, fortitude and would be able to work collectively in tough conditions. That is not to say that they were docile, and at different times, some of these strongly-willed individuals would challenge Shackleton's leadership.

Shackleton understood the threats to life of the Antarctic environment and adopted a command style of leadership. Even the ship's captain was subordinate to Shackleton, the expedition leader. Although in command, Shackleton would listen to the crew members discussing courses of action and after consideration would make final decisions. Also, Shackelton was not stubborn and would change a decision in the face of new information or changing circumstances. However, Shackelton did expect loyalty and commitment from his crew members, as he well understood that survival in The Antarctic depended on a concerted and sustained collective effort from all the team. Shackleton in his own actions focused the crew members on acting in the greater good of the group.

The Crew Manifest
Ernest Shackleton – Leader of the Expedition
Frank Wild – Second in Command
Frank A. Worsley – Captain of 'Endurance'
Frank Hurley – Official Photographer
Herbert Hudson – Navigating Officer
Lionel Greenstreet – First Officer
Tom Crean – Second Officer
Alfred Cheetham – Third Officer
Lewis Rickenson – Chief Engineer
Alexander Kerr – Second Engineer
James A. McIlroy – Surgeon
Alexander H. Macklin – Surgeon
Robert S. Clark – Scientist (Biologist)
Leonard D. A. Husssey – Scientist (Meteorologist)
James M. Wordie – Scientist (Geologist)
Reginald W. James – Scientist (Physicist)
George Marston – Official Artist
Thomas Orde-Lees - Motor Expert
Harry 'Chippy' McNeish – Carpenter

Charles Green – Cook
John Vincent – Able Seaman
Timothy Macarty – Able Seaman
Walter How – Able Seaman
William Bakewell – Able Seaman
Thomas McLeod - Able Seaman
William. Stephenson – Fireman, stoker
Ernest Holness – Fireman, stoker
Perce Blackborrow – Steward (boarded as a stowaway).

The Endurance sails to the Antarctic

The leader is dependent on followership and must have the character, competence and capability to succeed

The goal of the expedition was to cross Antarctica, the last uncharted continent, on foot. The name of their ship, which was built in Norway for polar voyages, was *Endurance*. Shackleton selected this name from part of his family motto: "Fortitudine Vincimus" (by Endurance we Conquer). The *Endurance* sailed from England in August 1914 just one month before Europe became entangled and immersed in World War I. This looming crisis hung over the heads of Shackleton, his crew, sponsors and the government. So much so, that Shackleton volunteered his entire crew to serve together if war broke out and queried whether he should call off the expedition.

Winston Churchill at the Admiralty promptly answered the response to his offer. The telegram said one word: "Proceed."

Endurance was readied to head South and then to the Pole. During his voyage he kept his personal communication of the voyage with his wife, Emily Dorman, on a regular basis. In his letters he recognized that he was an imperfect husband. Emily was a very strong woman and a great supporter. She was the vital link between Shackleton, the media and his sponsors to keep the pressure on these stakeholders while he was travelling to ensure success.

The ship arrived at South Georgia, a Whaling Station. Shackleton listened to local knowledge from the Norwegian whalers who knew Antarctic territory and polar sea conditions. They informed him of the worst ice in years and to hold off. Shackleton waited some weeks but decided to see for himself what the ice conditions were like.

In January 1915, after sailing for six weeks through 1,000 miles of pack ice and only a day's sail short of its destination, the *Endurance* was caught in a storm and pushed into the pack ice in the Weddell Sea where they became iced in.

This unforeseen setback was to be the beginning of an epic journey in which Shackelton was to adapt to changing circumstances to save his crew. This is a survival story of 50-foot waves and 50-knot winds. Norwegian mariners had a saying that at 40 degrees South there was no law and at 50 degrees South there was no God.

This leadership challenge would end after an incredible journey by Shackleton and his crew of 27, which included hauling by hand the three ship's boats on sledges over impossible frozen terrain, camping and drifting on ice floes, sailing the three boats to Elephant Island, building a survival camp shelter for the crew.

Shackleton realized that the full expedition was not capable of sailing further in the dangerous heaving stormy waters of the South Atlantic. Shackleton adapted his plans to take account of this the perilous context. He had the carpenter make the largest boat, the James Caird, ready to sail through the storm ridden waters. Shackleton set sail with Frank Worsley and four others, planning to cover 800 miles and reach the island of South Georgia. The sea journey was harrowing, with Worsley only able to take infrequent navigational readings in breaks in the weather. After 16 days of enduring tempestuous rain and storms, they landed on a beach in South Georgia. The boat was too battered to continue, and Shackleton decided to make a trek by foot for over 30 miles to reach a small whaling station. However, the natural environment posed a disturbing challenge. The whaling station was on the other side of the island and they would have to cross a 2,000-meter-high icy mountain range to reach it.

In an example of how Shackleton encouraged his crew to adapt to the context, Harry 'Chippy' McNeish, the carpenter, took two-inch brass screws from the boat and inserted them in the boots so that they would have a grip on the icy mountain sides. They had no tent or sleeping bags, and Shackelton knew that they would have to make the utmost haste without stopping in order to survive. After 36 hours of climbing stumbling, and eventually sliding down the other side of the mountain they reached the whaling station of Stromness on the other side of the island. Here Shackleton was able to obtain help and organize the eventual rescue of his crew.

This leadership journey took place in a context where leader and follower came face-to-face with survival and for some that is a belief in God. Shackleton had been raised as a Quaker and his faith resided in hope and that dedication to the task would ensure the guiding hand of Providence. He grew up in Ireland in a household of strong beliefs, strong women and strong ethos. This important aspect of his character will be detailed later.

Ambitions to reach the Pole and chart the last unknown continent flourished in a fertile public mind.

Shackleton's ambition to cross the South Pole arose in the specific social and political context of the time. In the spring of 1912, the world's attention turned to Antarctica. During this period, five major expedition formed, racing to be the first to the South Pole and the public and media were in a frenzy to ensure that their nation was first. Individuals of outstanding leadership experience, competence and capability emerged, including Scott and Shackleton of Britain, Amundsen of Norway, Shirase of Japan, Filchner of Germany and Mawson of Australia. Shackleton's story is set in a context of competition between colonial powers with the prize their national flag first to the Pole.

There was a contest for influence between blocs of powerful countries asserting their economic and political influence in the changing make-up of Europe. Adding to the forces of change are the evolution of new technology, the steam engine, telegraph, radio, and modern and powerful armaments of war with artillery and the machine gun to wreak havoc in an imminent war. The world was awakening from the old order, social stability and social constraint. Leadership itself was also changing

Our mental map can limit us taking bold steps in pursuit of extraordinary goals.

One's mental map of the world can have profound implications for what actions we take. Christopher Columbus obtained funding for an expedition of three ships to sail across the Atlantic believing that he would reach the coast of Japan and China, since Europeans had not discovered the Americas at that time. However, due to errors in interpreting older maps, he had grossly miscalculated the distance and instead of reaching East Asia, he reached several Caribbean islands. Even though his mental map was incorrect, it still provided him with the vision to sail across the Atlantic and explore territory unknown to Europeans.

Our consciousness of the world being a sphere was first articulated by Ptolemy and then by Aristotle who argued that Earth was a sphere and the center of the universe among the visible celestial bodies. It took until 1510 for Nicolaus Copernicus with handmade tools to map the night sky. He used complex mathematics to revolutionize our understanding of the cosmos by demonstrating that the earth was not the dominant sphere of our known universe. This work inspired Galileo who in 1612 published: *Dialogue Concerning the Two Chief Systems of the World*. His proposition was that the sun was the center of the universe. This heretical concept challenged Roman Catholic Church teachings and he spent the last decade of his life under house arrest.

Another example of shifting a mental map occurred when we saw the first photos of Earth from an Apollo space mission in the 1960s. Humanity saw itself for the first time as a fully illuminated orb, set amidst the darkness of space. Many have since echoed the words of Dave Scott, Apollo 9 and 15 missions, "It truly is an oasis — and we don't take very good care of it. I think the elevation of that awareness is a real contribution to saving the Earth". This re-drawing of our mental map spurred the environmental movement.

It has taken over two thousand years to learn that the old flat map of the universe is not the territory. It illustrates clearly that those who challenged accepted concepts were ahead of the curve. They were also often discounted and punished.

Maps and mindsets start in the imagination then shape reality.

The leader needs to have foresight, the vision to herald change and the ability to inspire people to adapt to new and emergent situations. The skill of a leader is to turn vision into reality and show followers a better way to succeed. Leadership requires the ability to recognize the inherent bias in old habits of the mind.

Adaptive change requires moving out of old habits and entering new, often daunting, territory. The starting place for the change journey is to understand the emerging context and be prepared to formulate objectives within that context. Understanding the context requires the leader to recognize the myths, maps, legacy systems and old narratives that impact and limit the ability to shape the context, leverage relationships and manage tasks.

Leadership requires the intelligence to challenge accepted mental maps and navigate the context for success. Leadership is enabling people to deal with changing situations and to be able to adapt to new environments. Responsible leaders enable people and communities to move to more adaptive and sustainable ways of dealing with changing settings, whether they are social, economic, political or environmental.

Chapter Summary

Leaders need to be able to understand the context, recognize leadership challenges and work with the group to act. Shackleton's epic story shows that leadership can be understood as lived experience, not just a theory.

Intelligence refers to the ability to understand and deal with new and trying situations. Psychologists have identified different types of intelligence and importantly leadership requires that several of these different intelligences need to work in unison. You have no doubt heard of IQ, which refers to one's intelligence for solving problems. IQ is an important predictor of leadership success, but also important is the leader's emotional intelligence (EQ) which is a capacity to understand and work with people. Additionally, there is a social intelligence (SQ) which refers to a capacity to work within social and institutional settings in a responsible and ethical manner. Leaders who can integrate effectively these three types of intelligence achieve a kind of super intelligence to inform self-awareness as a foundational state of mind and level of consciousness to move from the inner world to the outer social world context. Super-intelligent leaders are confident in their own ability and respect the feedback and advice of others. Followership is also not benign and should not be taken for granted.

Broader Reflection on the Challenge of Context.

It takes a courageous and informed leader to challenge the existing worldview and speak truth and be the change in the world. The lesson for the leader is to know the context and know how others see it.

To understand Shackleton's leadership context in 1912, there had been innovations and rapid industrialization changing the world. It was an age of autocratic leadership and submissive followership towards authority and institutions. It was a time of immense wealth, massive exploitation and dire poverty. It was an age where many were poorly educated with limited options who deferred to authority without question. Many shared a religious belief that required doing good unto others. Social norms were changing with the rise of the industrial class, state education, female emancipation and universal suffrage and organized challenges to the status quo in the form of trade unions.

Leadership occurs in a specific time and place. What works at one time, in one situation with a specific group, may not work in another context. Exemplary leaders, such as Shackleton, can generate a synergy and energy with engaged followers to achieve exceptional outcomes that were considered unattainable or even impossible.

A brilliant conductor can lift the performance of an orchestra to play superb music, military commanders rely on leadership to gain ascendancy on the battlefield. In business, the leader can generate interest and enthusiasm for a brand and product so that it becomes a household name.

Shackleton's Leadership Challenge: leading in a challenging crisis context.

Shackleton the leader is constantly faced with incredible challenges and changing crisis contexts. These unstable contexts at the edge of experience require the responsible leader to develop a state of mind that can adapt and re-align the expedition's strategic purpose to succeed together. Meeting the challenge of losing his ship and cut off from the rest of the world is not for the faint hearted. This is a wicked not tame problem. This context and challenge require utilizing all the 7 principles of leadership to ensure followers are committed to success not failure.

Contemporary Leadership Challenge – Case study leading in context:

In the working contexts and locales of operations where police, fire, health and uniform service professionals operate the context is constantly changing. These professional and skilled individuals are in advance briefed on the mission and objectives. In reality they find that the context changes constantly and unfolds literally before their eyes on the ground. Here is a classic case of the map not being the territory. To further compound their mission and objectives these professionals work with other agencies who often have a different interpretation of the mission to work in the context.

Responsible leadership requires clearly knowing the shared context, motives, countervailing values and perspectives of how diverse stakeholders interpret the mission, objectives and needs. Failure to manage in this shared context can result in unintended consequences such as increased conflict and crisis. An unprepared leader, to quote a serving police officer, can quickly see the leader go from hero to zero if not prepared. Working with professionals in defence, development and diplomacy in the complex context of a recent Afghanistan mission provides an excellent example of how leading in a context is challenging. For example, this is called a whole of government approach where agencies cooperate to help a failing state become stable. The hard lesson learned is that each of the agencies see context through a different lens. One context but three perspectives are the reality on the ground of diverse stakeholders not operating under the same rules. Good intentions in this context can quickly turn into unforeseen consequences and undetermined outcomes. This reality plays out in contexts where different entities vie for leadership, finances, control and resources. The responsible leader needs to know the shared objectives and the contextual challenge to survive and succeed.

Leadership Log – Principle 1: Understand the context.

In this chapter and the next we explore how the leader makes the connection between the inner world of one's habits of the mind (consciousness) and the constraints and opportunities of the external world (context). An important dimension of the external world involves the social dynamics around individuals and groups.

- Recognize a context is complex and the map is not the territory.

- Think of context as woven into the fabric of myth and belief

- Understand that stakeholders interpret context from tribal royalties.

- Be conscious that context is shaped by history, myth and legacy.

> *- Consider context as a layered map with fault lines to navigate.*
>
> *- Understand that successful leaders cultivate a shared narrative that creates people of the map and context.*
>
> *- Collaboratively understand countervailing values, perspectives and create dialogue to develop shared meaning and purpose.*

Self-assessment for self-mastery in understanding the context

- How does your mental map influence your understanding of people, places and problems?

- How has your self-reference criteria spurred unsatisfactory decisions and unintended consequences? What does it say about bias and misunderstanding in problem-solving and decision-making?

- How could you develop better understanding of a context to improve outcomes?

- What would help you at work in reshaping the context to succeed?

- Develop a leadership Log to track progress as your private journal to help retain and review key concepts of responsible leadership for self-mastery.

Chapter 2: Leadership Consciousness

THE MIND OF THE RESPONSIBLE LEADER

Shackleton crew member conscious of the crisis context and
unpredictable tasks ahead required to survive.
Painting by the author based on surviving photographic plates.

*"One feels 'the dearth of human words, the roughness of mortal speech' in
trying to describe things intangible."*
                                                            Ernest Shackleton.

THE SECOND PRINCIPLE – DEVELOP LEADERSHIP CONSCIOUSNESS

"Where there is no vision, the people perish: but he that keepeth the law, happy is he." - Proverbs 29:18

"I will not let anyone walk through my mind with their dirty feet." - Mahatma Gandhi

"There is no coming to consciousness without pain. People will do anything, no matter how absurd, in order to avoid facing their own Soul. One does not become enlightened by imagining figures of light, but by making the darkness conscious." - Carl Jung

"You are an explorer, and you represent our species, and the greatest good you can do is to bring back a new idea, because our world is endangered by the absence of good ideas. Our world is in crisis because of the absence of consciousness." - Terence McKenna

The lived voice of responsible leadership on consciousness. In developing a graduate leadership program, it was a good time to introduce innovative learning approaches that linked theory and practice. One approach was to have a cohort of professionals research the movie Gandhi and evaluate how the movie impacted their sense of consciousness and understanding. It was illuminating to find how the diverse multi-cultural cohort interpreted Gandhi and his non-violent approach for the struggle for Independence from different levels of understanding. Some from a British background expressed a sense of shame in his treatment and struggle. Others from an Indian background took a different approach thinking that Gandhi succeeded because he showed that a sense of fair play did not work both ways. Being conscious of differences and internal bias is part of being human. It requires that we need to understand the perspectives of others before being quick to judge others from our own state of consciousness.

Leadership consciousness refers to the leader's understanding of self and others in any context. In knowing thyself the leader will understand their own self-reference criterion (SRC). This involves knowing how they see things, how others see things and how the leader thinks others see the leader. Failure to be conscious of the SRC can impact and bias decision-making and relationships with followers. This will differ beyond culture as some cultures are high context such as Japan where the context shapes the decision-making more than in North America where the low context culture requires the emphasis on communication. This is a recipe for disagreement. Knowing whether the leader is working in a high or low context requires adjusting SRC to see beyond their comfort level or cultural norm. Consciousness involves a sense of understanding one's own humanity as well as that of others. Traditionally we have called this quality empathy. In recent scientific research the concept of emotional intelligence has been studied to explain how some leader are more successful at influencing followers. These concepts are all the same territory as the concept of leader consciousness. We are referring to the leader's capacity to manifest a sense of humanity in all their actions and to display a mature understanding of self and others.

A leader needs to be conscious of when to act with courage to tackle the messy problems to rebuild trust with followers. Shackleton demonstrated a clear grasp of the physical environment of the Antarctic and was able to understand the impact the life-threatening context on the social-team environment of the expedition members as well as the individual fears and anxieties of each expedition member.

CHALLENGE 2 - LEADERSHIP CONSCIOUSNESS FOR UNDERSTANDING

Leadership consciousness refers to the leader's understanding of self and others in a specific context. This understanding encompasses others' perceptions of the context, their feelings and emotions as well as the social interactions that take place in that context. Leadership consciousness refers to the capacity of the leader to manifest a sense of humanity in all actions and to display a developed understanding of self and others. The challenge for the leader is to be open and receptive to changing circumstances in the physical environment as well as the ever-shifting social dynamic of the group.

As a proven mariner, Shackleton knew that the crew lived in a 24/7 context, close quarters and no room for pretense or game playing. The pre-planning showed this level of conscious preparation and intelligence based on experience to provide the best chance for success. Shackleton had a clear understanding of the impact that the long dark polar winter would have on the psychological and physical wellbeing of the expedition members. In his record of events, Shackleton notes how the "disappearance of the sun is apt to be a depressing event in the polar regions" and that winter imposes both mental and physical stress. Shackelton encouraged the crew to conduct concerts at night and engage in games of amusement to keep up spirits and to pass the long hours of darkness.

A leader must provide strategic direction

Shackleton made exacting plans in preparation of the exacting travails of traversing the Antarctic continent. The ship *Endurance* was prepared, packed with provisions, the expedition members boarded, and then embarked with 69 dogs from Canada for work on the ice. Shackleton stayed behind to take care of final matters and the Endurance sailed off. He headed on another ship to South America to meet the Endurance in port.

On arrival he quickly learned of dissention among the crew and poor leadership. As the leader he quickly instituted his authority and dealt quickly with the crew that needed to be reprimand, including several being dismissed.

A leader needs the courage to tackle messy problems to rebuild authority, integrity and trust with followers. Shackleton turned a bad experience into a transformative experience for his followers. His crew respected his leadership and he was known by all as "Boss." This was not an authoritarian mantle but an authoritative mark of respect for his principled leadership and concern for followers.

Link to current Research

Working with people can be demanding, and leaders need to be able to put aside their own personal concerns and be on top of the fears and dreams of followers. Only by doing so, can one inspire others and lead them.

Consumer psychologists have noted the tendency of people to rely on their own cultural values and experiences as the basis for decision making and to evaluate others. Technically this tendency is called the Self-Reference Criterion (SRC). This tendency shapes perception and serves as a potential bias to distort or dismiss how we see and react to things. The SRC can be most pronounced when dealing with people outside our cultural experience and the typical distinctions would be around gender, class and race.

Given the composition of Shackleton's crew, the blind spot for Shackelton would have been most likely around class, that is, not understanding the motivations and aspirations of the men who had very different upbringings to Shackleton. Failure to be conscious of the SRC can impact on and bias problem-solving, decision-making and trusted relationships with followers.

The SRC can manifest as a potential leadership derailer when dealing with people from other cultures. These cultural differences can be a potential area for disagreement and pose potential mind-fields that can damage any potential collective action.

Regardless of diversity, other research has found that a capacity for emotional intelligence is important for positive interactions with others. Emotional intelligence refers to the individual's capacity to express emotion appropriately in the right context, and to manage interpersonal relationships in an empathetic manner. Research indicates that leaders with a higher capacity for emotional intelligence are more successful at influencing followers. A leader needs to be conscious of when to act with courage to tackle messy problems and rebuild trust with followers. Doing so involves knowing how they see things, how others see things and how the leader thinks others see the leader.

Knowing yourself as a leader, whether you are working in a high or low context requires adjusting the SRC to see beyond their comfort level or cultural norm. Importantly leaders need insight into knowing self and others and having a sense of humanity, emotional intelligence and empathy.

In the contemporary social and organizational context many people come from diverse cultures, faiths and beliefs. The challenge in leadership is to develop perspective and approaches to find common ground for cultivating trust and collaboration.

Leadership in Crisis

As well as dealing with crew matters, Shackleton was also conscious of the potential concerns posed by the climate and the weather. Ice floes were reported a long way north that summer and Shackleton discussed the ice conditions with the whalers who had experience of the Weddell Sea. He took on extra stores of clothing in case of being forced to stay a winter and decided to take extra coal stored on the deck of the Endurance, in case of heavy going through ice floes. Shackleton was conscious of the variability of the Antarctic weather and took precautions to provide himself with options depending on what weather prevailed.

The Endurance sailed towards the Weddell Sea, and encountered pack ice further north than Shackleton expected. They steamed through loose pack ice for a number of weeks and set the sails as well to save coal. On encountering gales, they would wait in the lee of a large iceberg, and once the gale had passed, they would look for open sea lanes between the ice bergs. After weeks of progress the Endurance hit an ice floe and became stuck. The crew lived on board, hunting seals for food, and making progress by drifting with the ice pack. Shackleton prepared the crew to endure a long winter on board the ship stuck in the ice.

In the spring the pressure of the ice increased, and Shackleton reports the deck shaking, the beams arching and the stanchions buckling. Shackleton prepares the crew to be ready to respond to any emergency. The thawing ice formed pressure ridges that started to crush the *Endurance*. Eventually the ice crushes the ship, and the deck started to break upwards as the water poured in below. Shackleton gives the order to abandon ship. He fully realizes that they have lost their home on the ice. They are disconnected from the world. They are perilously stuck in the ice and chances of survival are precarious at best.

Shackleton has prepared for this eventuality, and the crew shift the supplies and tents and other equipment from the ship onto the ice. Shackleton's strength of character and conscious state of mind, body and spirit in this crisis context rapidly build trust in his words, deeds and actions to reshape a desperate context to one where followers are resilient and optimistic to succeed as a team. He demonstrated a conscious understanding of the life-threatening challenges of the physical environment of the Antarctic and was able to understand the fears and anxieties of each expedition member.

Shackleton addresses the crew to ensure positive morale and shared purpose. Living on the shifting ice is an unnerving experience with the ice crushing and breaking under their feet. In a mark of poignant symbolism, they raise the flag on the ship as a mark of no surrender. He then makes another highly symbolic gesture and rips three pages from the Bible given him by the Queen and places the Bible to be left on the ice. This is leadership character by effect and sends a clear message that in order to survive only essential items may be kept.

In these conditions Shackleton needs to lead with decisive purpose to ensure crew cohesion is focused on the objectives of survival at all costs. His words, deeds and actions can either inspire or nurture doubt. He knows that responsible leadership must take decisive action to respond to the recent incident and raises his consciousness and state of mind as a leader to reshape the context and engage followers in the shared purpose of survival. It is all for one and one for all.

Crisis is a time for the leader of personal dead reckoning.

Shackleton is clear about his responsibility: "my thoughts flew round to the problem ahead. If the party had not numbered more than six men a solution would not have been so hard to find; but obviously the transportation of the whole party to a place of safety, with the limited means at our disposal, was going to be a matter of extreme difficulty".

The context of losing his ship and moving onto the polar ice leads to increased crew doubts about survival but Shackleton takes charge, leads and provides direction. He requires that all hands are on deck, no matter what position or rank, to get to the tasks at hand to survive. The ship's carpenter takes a less than positive outlook on the possibility of survival. Shackleton addresses the whole crew and any form of malcontent and dissention is swiftly addressed to ensure positive crew morale.

Living on the shifting ice is an unnerving time with the ice crushing and breaking under their feet. Frank Hurley the photographer who is akin to official storyteller captures the story as it unfolds. He relentlessly carries his heavy cumbersome photographic equipment everywhere to ensure an accurate record of events are kept for posterity as they unfold.

Later Shackleton thanked Hurley for saving the pictures. Without them all, we would be left with are words and sometimes these are not enough to tell the whole courageous story of survival. As they set-up camp on the ice, the ship let out its final death cry and sinks through the ice as though it had never existed. One can feel the tension and emotion in collectively watching the death of their ship and the context of safety and security from the ravages of the polar weather.

Back on the ice Shackleton keeps his crew busy with a multitude of tasks to keep them motivated. This includes revisiting the crushed ship daily to retrieve supplies before it slips beneath the water. This includes salvaging 72 hours worth of food supplies and retrieving the sledges, ships boats, equipment and the dogs.

Posterity was now being carried with them.

Frank Hurley, the official photographer, dives into the frigid hold to retrieve 300 plus cans of film to ensure the story survives. The crew is informed that they may only carry 33 pounds in weight the rest is to be left behind. Hurley played a vital role in capturing the unfolding story of the voyage on film in detail. He was meticulous in cataloguing the story. When the ship was crushed, he went back to the ship several times at great risk and dived into the ship to retrieve his precious film containers as he realized that without these there would be no story to tell and inspire future generations.

By the time the ship had been crushed and sank Hurley had retrieved over 200 containers of film. Shackleton said he could take 100. Hurley was persuasive and it was decided 150 would be carried, the best were selected the others left on the ice

The role of the storyteller as keeper of the story can be traced back to our historical communities in which it was not possible to maintain written records or where many people could not read or write. A ships' artist and photographer take on the role of the storyteller and are keepers of the flame. They help create the shared narrative, the myth and the collective memory that inspires, shapes identity and cultural belief. It is no wonder that Hurley fought hard to convince Shackleton to keep the film plates and drag them on the sledge across the polar ice.

In the contemporary organization the role of the storyteller is often sanitized and retold by PR to build a brand. This is not a true narrative account of the trials and tribulations that shape corporate legacy and it is a reason why legacy systems can surface in the future to sabotage or derail ambition and goals

The challenge of understanding the tough choices

Shackleton shows that a leader cannot afford to be sentimental in this survival context. A leader must be hard and decisive in order to show his leadership is determined to succeed. One of the first instructions he gives to the ship's carpenter is to shoot his pet kitten. Shackleton recognizes that as things are to deteriorate the dogs would have killed the kitten for food. He makes the hard decisions, so they all have a chance to live and not die.

The next stage of the journey of survival begins. This has been a chilling experience. They have lost their ship. They are disconnected from the world. They are perilously stuck on the unsafe polar ice and chances of survival are precarious at best. On the ice, Shackleton was well aware of the predicament of the expedition " One feels our helplessness as the long winter night closes upon us". In these conditions the leader needs to lead with principle and purpose. This is a context where walking the talk must happen.

At this point Shackleton's awareness of a solemn occasion draws on his love of poetry to express the moment. His timing as a leader is poignant and not wasted on the crew. He quotes lines from his favorite poet Robert Browning called Prospice....

> *"For sudden the worst turns the best to the brave,*
>
> *the black minute's at end."*

Shackleton's leadership character and state of mind to reshape the way in which the crew understands the context communicates hope with the efficacy aimed at achieving a specific objective. As a leader he changes the context to make the crew resilient and optimistic to succeed.

Know Thyself: The conscious step to responsible leadership.

Preparing leaders to journey to an awareness of self where heart, mind and spirit lead to authenticity, humility and trust is a painful migration. The ancient Greek storytellers understood well this state of mind. Homer in the Odyssey links the leadership learning journey to an awareness of self. Many prominent leadership researchers view leadership as an ongoing journey that requires constant and ongoing personal attention to one's own state of mind and personal development.

The fragmented context of the contemporary world requires deep self-reflection and an enlightened perspective to understand the complexity of change and to recognize new approaches to emergent and tough problems. Leaders are likely to find the old maps to be misleading, the legacy systems obsolete and that there is little coherent understanding in community. This challenge to leadership pushes the leader to rely on their strength and capacity of their own consciousness.

Historically, navigators on the ocean could find themselves in situations where the storms and clouds blanketed out all celestial navigational signs, the sun, moon or stars and they had to rely on a practice known as dead reckoning. In these situations, the navigator would calculate a dead reckoning of current location based on last observed position and estimation of courses steered and distances run. Today, ship's radar and GPS systems can fail, and again the navigator might have to rely on dead reckoning. For a leader, a personal dead reckoning occurs when a course has to be set, and there are no clear sign posts of where they will end up.

Every leader has at one time gone through this type of personal dead reckoning and soul searching. The need for perspective and insight is pivotal to understand the context and people that shape actions.

Leadership might be about action and influencing others, but at its core it depends on a leader who has a robust and strong enough personality to handle setbacks and criticisms. The themes of self-knowledge and self-reverence are important in the research on the healthy personality. These themes have been of interest to poets and writers who have thought deeply about the human condition. For instance, in his famous poem *Oenone*, Tennyson (1832) identifies the strength that comes from of self-reverence, self-knowledge and self-control.

> *Kept watch, waiting decision, made reply.*
> *Self-reverence, self-knowledge, self-control,*

> *These three alone lead life to sovereign power.*
> *Yet not for power (power of herself*
> *Would come uncall'd for) but to live by law,*
> *Acting the law we live by without fear;*
> *And, because right is right, to follow right*
> *Were wisdom in the scorn of consequence.*
>
> *Tennyson, Oenone.*

Tennyson invites us to reflect on important things about knowing thyself. These words act as a mirror held up to the leader to assess conscious preparedness to lead others. With few exceptions the leaders of organizations that get into serious trouble lack one or more of Tennyson's three characteristics of self. Tennyson's poem teaches a 'trinity of excellences' of self-reverence, self-knowledge and self-control that help us understand the consciousness that help one know thyself in any context.

The leadership definition of the principle of consciousness has profound implications.

The leader needs to be conscious of the context, the relationships and the tasks required as well as the leader's own preferences, bias or inhibitions to any action. Misreading or misunderstanding of these relationships can have fatal consequences. Consciousness enables the leader to understand when to act with courage to tackle messy problems. Shackleton demonstrated a clear grasp of the physical environment of the Antarctic and was able to understand the impact the life-threatening context on the social-team environment of the expedition members as well as the individual fears and anxieties of each expedition member. Leadership consciousness goes beyond empathy. Although understanding and sharing the emotions of others is a foundational aspect of what we mean as leader consciousness.

Other important components of leadership consciousness relate to being able to understand the likely effects any envisaged action will have on followers. Shackleton demonstrated clear consciousness of the extreme danger posed by the Antarctic environment to both the physical and mental survival of the expedition members, as well as the limitation and strengths of his own leadership capacity. He was aware of the impact of the life-threatening context on the social-team environment of the expedition members as well as the individual fears and anxieties of each expedition member. Furthermore, he was able to envisage ways to counter these threats and implement action in a way that strengthened the trust between him and the crew.

Legacy maps, that is looking to the past, can inhibit innovation and thinking for the future horizon and future success. A leader needs to consider events as they unfold and be prepared for the unexpected.

Implications for responsible leadership.

Leadership that lacks awareness of the principle of consciousness is open to the changing winds of opportunism and the dangerous law of unintended consequences. Responsible leadership is required to avoid the harsh pitfalls of the contemporary context that have resulted in financial, social, economic, political conflict and crisis. Many leaders work in contexts and climates that they think they understand but in reality, they lead in a hidden unconscious organizational sub-context that is shaped by the past and legacy systems rarely spoken of as they would unlock past challenges that could be hard to manage. This sub-conscious world is one where the archetypal ravines, currents and thin ice lurk that have the potential to sink leadership objectives and planned for outcomes.

The need for perspective is pivotal to understand context, beliefs, ideology and actors that shape actions. The challenge is to develop the perspective and leadership approaches to find common ground for cultivating trust and collaboration for the common good. It often takes a crisis to act and do the right thing. The contemporary context is laden with crises. In an inter-connected world these are complex and multi-layered. This is a context where leadership will be continuously challenged and tested. It requires leaders with resilience, stamina, courage and fortitude. It requires character. It involves sacrifice. It requires rigor in prior learning and practice in implementation.

Legacy emphasis on the individual leader

Leadership in the past was studied and practiced with a focus on the individual leader in an organization. This leadership mindset perceived the leader at the top of an organizational hierarchy with followers at the bottom. Top-down thinking has deep roots. It evolved in the DNA of the tribe, the clan and is evident in filial loyalty of master and servant relationships. Thinking such as this became embedded in military and monastic organizations and in organizational structure and strategy.

These formidable cultural maps helped shape the medieval mind and influence archetypes of leadership, ethos, structure and strategy in organization that still exist. The medieval mind was cultivated with a rigid schooling of grammar, logic, rhetoric, arithmetic, music, geometry, astronomy, physics and theology as the queen of the sciences. In the industrial mechanistic era, the leadership mind shifted to be underpinned by scientific rational determinism and mechanistic thinking of top-down, command and control. Schooling emphasized rational deterministic thinking to fit the machine age. The industrial mind was instructed with a curriculum of reading, writing and arithmetic to foster the industrial culture of time, technic and logic of know how in favor of know why. This worked for industrial production of workers on a production line. It fails to measure what matters for principled leadership and that is the recognition of the moral purpose and human side of enterprise.

Leaders who have managed tame problems are unlikely to be prepared for wicked problems of war, famine, disease, disaster, social-economic and political-environmental crisis. It will require exceptionally resilient leaders who are schooled in the importance of a responsible ethos that values new mental models for sense-making, and non-cognitive leadership competencies to mobilize followers who are willing to follow. It will take intelligence to reshape the context into one of hope and opportunity. The responsible leader needs to be a master of reading the context and shaping the context. This leader will understand the importance of building trust, transparency and acccuntability. The leader will have the strategic intelligence capability to identify and implement new emergent approaches for collaboration and cooperation.

In practice leadership is about life itself.

When leaders face problems, they face life in complexity, not compartmentalized packages of life. The best leaders possess wisdom, which is the ability to make the connection to transfer knowledge and make the best use of it. This capacity has important implications for leadership development that requires both tacit and explicit learning, which means that some of it cannot be coded or taught formerly.

Personal presence in leadership is a vital attribute especially in a crisis context. Leaders are not only shaped by environment; they also take active roles in remaking that environment in productive ways. In other words, exceptional leaders create contexts that support the exercise and cultivation of leadership. Shackleton found himself in a crisis context and was able to draw on his experience and wisdom to provide the crew with an inspired understanding of what they needed to do to survive.

In leading an organization, the followers are not passive, their knowledge and narrative build the distinct culture and capability. The very essence of dialogue (literally, dia-logos, flow of meaning) consists in mutual perspectives, which allows for, indeed promotes, the movement of followers into leadership roles. Leaders do not command simply by issuing unilateral directives. Instead leadership almost always involves cooperation and collaboration. These activities can only succeed in a culture that is founded on the core values of trust, integrity and confidence.

Institutional learning has been well developed. Lacking is the integration of collective wisdom often devalued by professions founded on specialization. Leadership for human development requires learning and connecting with collective wisdom often found in tribal, indigenous and communal cultures. In the past, some leaders have used visions and dreams to mobilize the will of the people to disastrous outcomes.

Responsible leaders need to understand that these legacy systems and mental models have been used as tipping points to mis-lead followers and take them over the cliff of destruction. In this time of inter-connectedness and interdependency a culture of leadership would support collaboration, consensus building and a social contract for common good. Collective wisdom informs us that this path is not without its own danger. The culture of responsible leadership is not one of cults, dogma or dictate. The wisdom and teachings found in each chapter provide examples of how to develop reflection, perspective and insight to wisely lead and excel in this new territory. The unethical leader on the other hand has abdicated responsibility. Others are in denial looking at mental maps of how to measure short-term that does not fit the contemporary context. It is time to roll-up this map.

At times we will find that we are at a moral and ethical crossroads on the leadership journey. Some leaders are profiting, many followers are stymied or suffering in unhealthy and toxic environments. Rewarding toxic leadership and acts of hubris, ego-gratification and self-preservation has moral and ethical consequences. These acts erode trust, loyalty and behavior of followers. It is time to take the responsible principled leadership path if we are to engage people to become resilient and sustain a healthy society founded on trust and hope.

Chapter Summary

The leader needs to have the strategic intelligence to identify and implement new approaches for collaboration and cooperation. Leaders have conviction and personal ambitions. Leadership is about doing the right thing. Whereas management is about doing things right. It is a set of competencies for planning, organizing, controlling and staffing. The leader requires both leadership and management competencies and that requires a developed state of mind. Leadership is a social construct embedded in culture, profession and identity. In a world beyond borders both mental, professional and geographic it is time to re-examine and advance a responsible leadership ethos to reduce the trust deficit and develop approaches for a moral enlightened ethos that cultivates trust, integrity, service, stewardship, collaboration and sustainability. It is a life-long pursuit. It is not simply an intellectual pursuit. It requires heart, mind and spirit to engender a serving ethos in life, in profession, community and vocation. It is a reflective mindset, enlightened ethos and strategic leadership ability that exudes confidence and positive energy in words, acts and deeds for transformation. It respects the reality that in the new contemporary context "we work together or whither together."

The need for taking the path less travelled to cultivate responsible leadership, talent, ethos, harmony and purpose is an ethical imperative. In an age of soft power with an increase in crises, competition, national self-interest and fueled by information and disinformation the leader with the consciousness, intelligence and perspective to recognize exigencies and tipping points in the context and find approaches to navigate success will be leading others at the edge of experience.

Shackleton's Leadership Challenge: leading with consciousness of engaging followers.

Shackleton the conscious leader has developed the insight to understand that followers are not a benign group. Followers are at a heightened consciousness of the ship sinking and being in a crisis context and this impacts morale. The conscious leader listens to concerns, addresses them and projects responsible leadership and moral authority in words and actions to ensure the whole crew motivation is focussed on the shared objective of survival.

Contemporary Leadership Challenge – Case study leading with consciousness.

A leader who does not walk the talk soon loses the moral authority to lead others. This is evident when the leader advances personal or hidden agendas that undermine trust in and across the organization. Unconscious ego-driven leadership creates a toxic environment that ignores followers at their peril. Much of the contemporary financial crisis has its roots in unconscious leadership that leads to hubris and does not serve with integrity.

Working with professionals in the corporate sector it is interesting to see how some managers who are highly qualified on paper lack realistic understanding of the need to be aware of what Carl Jung termed the conscious and the unconscious in the organizational culture. As a senior consultant stated: "what gets you hired (credentials) can also get you fired (ethos)." We refer here to intellectual knowledge and emotional intelligence. One is work skill smart the other is people skill smart. Many things are conscious such as capability and can be learned. The unconscious is the shadow. It is the elephant in the boardroom. It is the nine tenth of the iceberg that can sink the best laid plans. It is recognized in political agendas, silent sabotage, insider knowledge and unspoken communications.

The challenge of leadership consciousness is in knowing thyself in words, deeds and action to project a level of informed self-confidence that communicates trust and informed awareness. The Latin maxim says it best: "what you are shouts aloud. I cannot hear what you say." To serve and lead responsibly requires an attuned state of consciousness and awareness of the unconscious in the organization that can derail.

Leadership Log - Principle 2: Leadership Consciousness

Developing the conscious state of mind for decision-making and problem solving.

---

1. *Know Thyself recognize what you stand for as a leader.*
2. *Self Reference Criterion can bias understanding and decision-making.*
3. *Strategic focus for leadership action and direction.*
4. *Informed perspectives support shared understanding for trust building.*
5. *Intelligent insight for collective sense making.*
6. *Moral ethical spectrum for decision-making.*
7. *Cognitive intelligence for context mapping.*
8. *Emotional intelligence for mobilizing collaboration.*
9. *Responsible leadership ethos for serving and sustaining.*

Self-assessment for self-mastery

Complete an honest assessment in your leadership log of truly knowing yourself by reflecting on the above nine points to improve your leadership state of mind.

"No! let me taste the whole of it, fare like my peers The heroes of old, Bear the brunt, in a minute pay glad life's arrears of pain, darkness and cold."

Browning..

Chapter 3: Leadership Character
Mind, Body, Spirit and Return On Integrity
CHARACTER, ETHOS, TRUST AND INTEGRITY

Shackleton's strength of character is seen here encouraging his crew to harness mind, body and spirit to haul the ship's boat across the ice to reach the open sea. This requires all hands on deck.

Painting by author based on surviving photographic plates.

"I chose life over death for myself and my friends...I believe it is in our nature to explore, to reach out into the unknown. The only true failure would be not to explore at all."   Ernest Shackleton.

THE THIRD PRINCIPLE - LEADERSHIP CHARACTER TO BE TRUSTED

"Nearly all men can stand adversity, but if you want to test a man's character, give him power." - Abraham Lincoln

"Whoever is careless with the truth in small matters cannot be trusted with important matters" - Albert Einstein

"Character cannot be developed in ease and quiet. Only through experience of trial and suffering can the soul be strengthened, vision cleared, ambition inspired, and success achieved." - Helen Keller

"The value of life lies not in the length of days but in the use you make of them; he has lived for a long time who has little lived. Whether you have lived enough depends not on the number of your years but on your will." – Montaigne.

The lived voice responsible leadership on character - *Captain Robert Falcon Scott the Antarctic explorer wrote that there was no way of life is 'quite so demonstrative of character as that which we had on these expeditions. One sees a remarkable reassessment of values... Here the outward show is nothing, it is the inward purpose that counts' (Scott Journals 5th May 1911.).*

Character plays an important role in shaping leadership values and virtues. A leader can suddenly find that their world has been turned upside down. Shackleton had set out to lead an expedition to the South Pole, but his ship, the Endurance, becomes trapped in the pack ice and a frantic effort to cut a path through is not successful. The ship is stuck, and the sheer pressure of the ice eventually will crush the ship. The mission is at a critical crossroads a crucial point calling for decisive leadership and decision-making to shift from failure to success. Being able to make this transformation requires a deep sense of knowing thyself. It means knowing your mind, body and spirit to serve, lead and excel no matter what the context. Shackleton's character was forged and stamped by his upbringing and experience. His values, his faith is manifest in his ethos (credibility), pathos (persuasiveness) and logos (inductive reasoning). His character is of quiet heroic stoicism that projects self-awareness, self-confidence and self-control.

CHALLENGE 3 - LEADERSHIP CHARACTER TO SERVE AND LEAD

Character is typically seen as the sum of qualities that defines a person, or the essence of a person. As the person can be perceived as good or bad, character is endowed with a strong moral dimension. Even though some research indicates that leadership might be defined in a social context and to some extent to be situationally determined, the character of the leader remains fundamental to achieving results with followers. The challenge of character for an individual is being able to cope with pressures and ethical demands of being a leader.

Character is key to the foundation of leadership. Character for leadership requires a deep sense of knowing oneself. It means knowing your mind and spirit to serve, lead and excel no matter what the context. Character shapes the values, virtues and actions that define one's leadership. It is at the foundation of living by the golden rule of treating others as you would wish to be treated. It is not for the faint hearted or one seeking to please others.

PERSONAL CHARACTER BUILDS TRUST

Character is evident in personal conviction in the confidence to serve and lead. Character is anchored in ethos, beliefs, integrity and values that shape our core identity and core purpose to lead.

Shackleton's character was forged and stamped by his upbringing and experience. In the contemporary context with the decline of deference, loss of institutional memory and changing social norms the exemplary leader of character must evolve from family, school and social institutions that believe in the virtue of decent behavior and fair play for all.

Today in a diverse society there is no overriding institution or national characteristic role model of expected norms. Principled norms must be mentored in words and actions by the leadership and distinct culture of an organization. Unfortunately, the importance of character development in leadership has been severely undermined by the corporate metrics of reward that seem to be exploited by toxic and unethical leaders. Rather than seeing character as a cornerstone of leadership, toxic leaders rely on manipulation and intimidation. The absence of leadership character at the top and a bad organisational culture encourage mimetic toxic learning within an organization. To avoid toxic leadership the responsible leadership character in an organization exemplifies positive leadership based on a code of conduct, recruits the right people and rewards expected behavior.

Leadership Character and Inner Voice of Experience.

Shackleton's character is of quiet heroic stoicism that projects self-awareness, self-confidence and self-control. Shackleton responds to the dramatic incident of losing his ship with decisive leadership character and competence. This is where his leadership character is tested, and he must be seen as trustworthy for followers to support and follow. Shackleton's strength of character and state of mind build trust and integrity in words and actions to reshape a desperate survival context to one where followers are resilient and optimistic to succeed as a collective team. Shackleton asserts his leadership character by overcoming crew dissention by clarifying a shared sense of purpose and tending to the needs and anxieties of his crew so that they come to believe in Shackleton as a leader worthy of their trust and support.

Shackleton had set out to lead an expedition to the South Pole, but his ship, the Endurance, becomes trapped in the pack ice and a frantic effort to cut a path through is not successful. The ship is stuck, and the sheer pressure of the ice eventually will crush the ship. The mission is at a critical crossroads calling for decisive leadership and decision-making to shift from imminent failure to success. Being able to make this transformation requires a deep sense of knowing thyself. It means knowing your mind, body and spirit to serve, lead and excel no matter what the context.

It is an exceptional leader who can admit to seeing failure as opportunity for leadership development. It says much about Shackleton. He was a fighter, afraid of nothing and no one. He was humane, kind, generous of spirit, affectionate and loyal to the wellbeing of his crew who all survived ten harsh months on the ice all being rescued.

It was Shackleton's character and conscious awareness of leadership that provided the example of trust and integrity required of all the crew to follow. His mind had been shaped by his upbringing and service as a mariner and crewmember on prior expeditions.

Ernest Shackleton was born in Kilkea. County Kildare, Ireland in 1874 (the same year as Winston Churchill). Ernest grew up in a Quaker household of strong beliefs, strong women and strong ethos. He was part of the Protestant Ascendancy, the descendants of English settlers who recognized Ireland not as a separate country but as a colony of the crown. Yet still very much the Irishman. His traits seem to illustrate persuasiveness, plausibility and a capacity to hide shrewd calculation under his outer charm. His father qualified as a medical doctor from Trinity College and his mother cared for the Shackleton brood of eight children six daughters and two sons. They moved to suburban London, England and enjoyed a comfortable life.

Ernest was accepted into the Mercantile Marine and at 16 he sailed from Liverpool to Valparaiso in the square-rigged sailing ship Houghton Tower. The ship was a three-mast clipper with full canvas and many sail lines to master. He literally learned the ropes the hard way as a mariner. He sailed round Cape Horn several times, once in the middle of the Southern winter, and earned the rank of second mate. Within four years after that he qualified as a certified master able to command a British ship on any sea. In 1897 he met Emily Dorman the daughter of a prosperous solicitor and fell in love. They both admired the poems of Robert Browning, which he quoted often. The classics and poetics still had a strong influence on the shaping of service, leadership and moral ethos in this era.

In 1899-1900 he served on ships transporting troops to the Boer War in South Africa. This was the time of the death of Queen Victoria and the end of her reign. Imperial destiny was in question and the ascendancy of the United States and tales such as Teddy Roosevelt's Roughriders and the Alaskan and Yukon gold rush were in the minds of those seeking new horizons. Shackleton sought a new path to experience adventure. In 1900 he heard about the National Antarctic Expedition the first British venture to the far south in 60 years. He befriended members of the Royal Geographical Society and was selected to join the expedition. However, as he was a Merchant marine officer, he did not take command. This responsibility went to a Royal Naval officer Robert Falcon Scott. From here on at the age of 27 the names of Shackleton and Scott would vie for leadership and Antarctic destiny in life and death. His first voyage to Antarctica did not fare well. He fell ill and Scott had him invalided home. He returned home disappointed with few prospects and no job. He had experience failure.

Failure can be a great teacher for a leader with vision and determination. Eventually Shackleton lead his own expedition to the Antarctic and in doing so became Scott's rival. Vision alone did not enable Shackleton to succeed, as well he needed a viable plan to obtain support and funding from wealthy patrons.

We see in Shackleton a leader with a sense of mission and destiny living in a social, political and technological context at a time of peace and certainty just before World War I when the tipping points of history and the tectonic plates of politics and social upheaval turned their world upside down. The year is 1912. The world is still at peace. It is the calm before the storm.

Leadership character and the role of ethos, pathos, logos.

A source of inspiration to understand the character of leadership is in reading the myths, literature and narratives of history's exemplary leaders. These principled leaders are iconic. The very name of leaders such as Horatio Nelson, Abraham Lincoln, Florence Nightingale, Mahatma Gandhi, Nelson Mandela and others bring forth images and stories of profound examples of leadership with character. Icons are objects worthy of veneration but not worship. Every leader is human and will have his or her share of human faults and frailties. These famous leaders can provide inspiration and can provide real life lessons, rather than being objects of vernation. The leadership stories found in literature provide words, deeds and images evident in the myths and oral traditions that nourished our ancestors. They are narratives worthy of being passed on as beacons of the best of the human spirit.

The story of Mahatma Gandhi provides a narrative around how non-violence was a powerful means to an end in the struggle for independence. His example provides a lesson on how the spirit and presence of a leader can confront the power of an empire and lead people to freedom and independence. The civil rights advocate, Martin Luther King Jr, who was a great communicator, moved people at a deep emotional level to invoke a sense of what is right and what is required of a leader in a challenging context.

The character of leadership embodied in Ernest Shackleton's epic Antarctic voyage is one of leadership character, courage and conviction. He was a leader of exceptional ability and respected by his crew. Stories provide profound leadership lessons of the importance of character and capability. His beliefs underpin the exemplary character of leadership. Leadership education is life-long, and narratives of leadership help foster a love of learning and inquiry. This learning leads to a fertile mind, greater reflection and perspective to revisit, rethink and reshape contexts and provide followers with hope. Leadership character refers to the need to shape leadership in the external world and succeed.

Although there is no single recipe list for the personal qualities required of a leader, certain key leader characteristics emerge from all the leadership research. Importantly the leader needs to be able to guide the right action in social contexts (ethos), connect with people at a fundamental emotional human level (pathos) and demonstrate that he or she has a viable grasp and understanding of the key dynamics of a situation and can acquire appropriate understanding as required (logos). Developing and practising these fundamental leadership characteristics will result in positive leadership outcomes of Hope, Efficacy, Resilience, and Optimism. The leader as hero redefined as more stoic and resilient leader not a conquering HERO.

The leadership principle of character refers to qualities that make a leader authentic and different from others. These are a combination of both nature and nurture that result in the strength and originality in a leader's nature. He had the strength of character to lead in adversity, with resilience and courage against odds of survival. Shackleton's leadership journey to the Antarctic provides a context to consider leadership as archetype and metaphor when understanding principled responsible leadership in specific contexts.

In the Antarctic expedition he and his crew walked over the water. How is this possible? The mind of the leader enabled him to see things that others do not see. Water takes many forms it is fluid and once frozen it becomes as hard as steel. The iceberg is a useful metaphor for illustrating leadership character. The iceberg is nine tenths below the surface. One tenth is visible. It is the hidden part that can sink a ship. The base of the archetypal iceberg is the character, the middle is competence and the visible is the capacity.

Every leader is different. To understand an individual leader or a distinct context the self-reference criterion of the observer must be aware of individual bias and filters that mis-interpret the leader or the context being assessed. The foundation of leadership is anchored in character and grounded in a serving ethos. Leadership development requires deeper understanding and to advance an enlightened leadership ethos requires informed thinking and courageous action to make bold moves to a new way of seeing things.

Cultivating Leadership Character, Ethos and Presence.

A crucial aspect of character is that of the moral component. Typically, when we refer to character, we think of virtues such as empathy, honesty, loyalty. fortitude and courage. Character is forged through life events and experiences. Importantly the leader needs to be aware of the ethical implications of any ethical challenges arising from the context and the associated ethical implications of any envisaged course of action. Although character is important, the leader needs to develop a robust ethical framework as leadership involves working in situations where alternatives are contested, and values can be conflicting.

In practice, leadership involves facing some obvious fundamental challenges: motivating followers; mobilizing their knowledge, skills, and abilities; creating and implementing an organizational vision; and managing change. A simple universal recipe for overcoming these challenges, however, has been elusive. Truly exceptional leaders have often assumed almost mythic, "iconic" status, their decisions not entirely explainable by ordinary people. In response, various schools of thought have arisen as to how leadership can be explained, and how it should be exercised, conceptualized and even defined. Each of these theories has implications for the understanding and practice of leadership. In a globalized world, belief systems shape countervailing differences in what is considered moral and ethical. The responsible leader will need to put on their armor of consciousness, character, confidence and courage to succeed. They need to remember that Shackleton's strength of character reshaped a desperate context into a context that made the crew resilient and optimistic to succeed.

Leadership is not about hubris and ego – it is about character and humility.

The word character derives from the Greek *kharakter* – a stamping tool. A way of understanding the importance of leadership character is to imagine a single piece of metal type used on a printing press. This single character is made of lead, tin and antimony. These three ingredients give it strength and endurance to survive a heavy pounding from the press. Human character development is similar. It needs to be made of elements that give it the strength of character for endurance to survive the daily pounding of serving and leading.

Shackleton's upbringing was the foundation from which he developed strength of character in words, deeds and actions. Shackleton's character was shaped by his family upbringing and Quaker roots. In Christian belief the three intertwined cords of faith, hope and charity speak to the character of a responsible servant leader. By the by, it is an interesting scientific fact three intertwined cords actually make the strongest possible cord. These foundational character traits shape an individual's sense of identity, belief and motivation. The ancient Greeks clearly understood this reality and defined the foundation in becoming a respected educated leader required developing ethos, pathos and logos. In contemporary language this translates as:

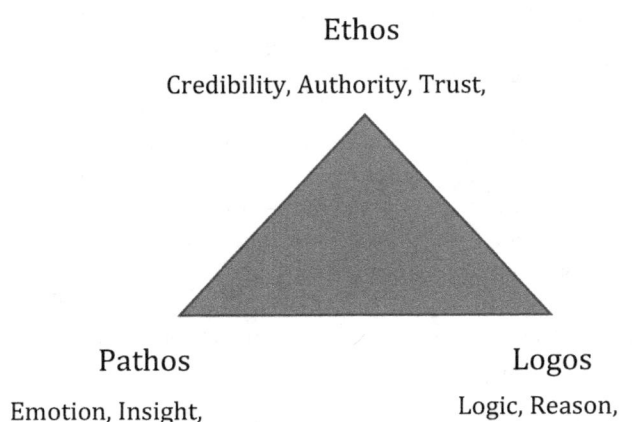

Figure 1. Ethos, Pathos and Logos: Responsible Leadership - Moral Purpose in Action

Ethos representing moral purpose and ethics in individual character for credibility of the leader to build trust and the ability to ethically persuade.

Pathos is the ability to appeal to emotion as a way of convincing follower's argument by creating an emotional response.

Logos is an appeal to logic and a way of persuading followers by use of reason.

Looking back to Shackleton's time, ethical conduct, emotional argument, rhetoric and logical dialectic were regarded as part of an educated mind. The universities and schools of Shackleton's era embraced a curriculum anchored in the ethos of service complemented by a requirement for proficiency in reading, writing, rhetoric and arithmetic.

The virtues of a fair go for all in shaping leadership behavior.

Often missed is the historic role of sports in education of the leader that were not simply for physical education as they embodied codes of conduct and fair play. Fair play is evident in games that evolved from the great schools such as Rugby school and cricket, which emerged on the village green a collective community. Cricket is not a democratic game. It installs strict codes of behavior and requirement for fair play by all and adjudicated by an umpire. It is often said the Battle of Waterloo was won on the playing fields of Eton.

Increasingly the sports ethos funded by professional interests is now focussed on a battle for competition between winners and losers. Character development does not evolve in a vacuum. It has been cherished in the development of the child, in the home, in the school, the church, social organizations and seen as a mark of decency and honor.

The ancient Greeks understood that leadership is not simply an intellectual pursuit but required development of a healthy mind and healthy body. Present leadership development is heavily focused on psychology, organizational and human resource management schools of thought. These outwardly fulfil learning of the practice of leadership. However, lacking is a deeper inner understanding of the character and ethos of responsible leadership. Our understanding of this inner character has evolved over centuries. Every culture and every generation has sought its own understanding of leadership. This comment implies leadership learning is best understood in context, time and place.

The first nations indigenous peoples of the world have very clear mental maps that are communicated through oral tradition. The shared narrative creates meaning. It is filled with myth, belief and narrative that shapes the character and ethos of leadership within the tribe. This use of narrative is not dissimilar to the story announced by the leader of the organization, the leader of a nation or the leader of an ideology. Cultivating leadership education in character and ethos requires more than a set of courses and competencies. It requires leaders to be authentic. Those who have inner strength, insight and inspiration to ignite the human spirit to reach their true potential will serve as exemplary leaders.

Leadership character is anchored in the golden rule of doing the right thing.

Morality is the precept of behavior founded on the tenets of religion or philosophy. Ethics is the accepted standard of behavior evident in the behavior of professions who accept a code of ethics to guide accepted behavior. The leadership prism for interpreting this complex moral spectrum is to understand the role that values play in interactions. Values are manifest in a sense of fair play, a fair go for all, treating others with respect. Values are evident in a corporate credo, religious creed and military esprit de corps. For the responsible leader to act ethically and be socially responsible differs in interpretation in cultures and professions. This reality is a leadership mind-field and in diverse contexts that are conflicting, fractured or broken it is difficult to predict outcomes.

Responsible leadership requires doing things right that must be done. The concept of *Must be Done* is stated in the mission within a legal framework. The leadership challenge in the socially responsible realm of ethics and obligations is that there are many messy issues about what might or should be done. Without good governance, accountability and transparency this messiness creates a fertile context for unethical leadership and subsequent harmful decisions. This messy domain is where the responsible leader should take a hard look in the mirror. It is a meeting place where truth and treachery co-exist. Where the responsible leader needs to know thyself and know thy context. The leadership deficit of non-compliance and silent sabotage is at work in this domain. It is evident in managing numbers and cutting people. It fosters mis-information, mendacity and breaking trust. Hubris often becomes its nemesis. The nexus of leadership, trust and followership can be quickly destroyed. In turn this undermines cohesion and weakens professional ethos. The challenge is about persuading people with egos and agendas to do the right thing. Leadership character and ethos are evident in personal conviction and confidence to lead. Without leadership character and leadership ethos the factors of competence and capability are rudderless. Character is anchored in ethos, beliefs and core values that shape core identity and core purpose. It is authentic. It is trusted. It has integrity. Leadership character is the hidden part of the metaphorical iceberg. It is not seen, yet it is real. It is the hidden location of integrity. It is the domain of emotional intelligence. It is manifest in behavior. It is the nexus between emotional intelligence and social intelligence. It informs the habits of mindset that impact follower relationships.

Leadership character is impacted by personal identity which is shaped by culture, mindset, language and sense-making.

The impact of identity and sense making is evident in shaping of the mind and world-view. The language of decision-making creates cultural and esoteric mindsets with which to make sense of contexts. A simple literal reductionist perspective ignores the nuance of verbal and non-verbal communications that exists in the locales of operation. Developing the responsible leadership state of mind requires being aware of bias and the nuances inherent in communications. A leader requires the rational mind for logic and the intuitive mind to interpret non-verbal communications found in contexts. There is no such thing as not communicating.

Presence such as boots on the ground communicates a specific message: an example of leadership by effect. The show of force achieves the goal by not using force. The "cold war" is an example of this reality. Threat of annihilation led to increased communication. This shifted the Internet as a technology of war to one of trade and social media. This has evolved to underpin the ascendancy of soft power to leverage influence and power. Research posits that the cultural mind exhibits masculine and feminine traits. Power and conquest illustrate high masculine traits. On the other hand, rapprochement, détente, consensus is an example of high feminine traits. The leadership mind needs to understand the context of operation and cultural identity of stakeholders to develop perspective in sense-making constructive dialogue (dia-logos – shared meaning) in specific contexts. Benefits of a responsible leadership character for developing leadership capacity to engage followership in the contemporary context include:

- Building trust, integrity and accountability.

- Fostering shared dialogue, to create common ground, understanding and the strengthening of collaboration around a shared sense of mission.

What responsible leadership identity and mindset is not about is a self-serving perspective. Keeping teams working together and staying in a positive frame of mind is a tough ask for the leader. Just reflecting on how the crew of the Endurance worked together to operate as a functioning team is an amazing outcome. An important factor here was Shackleton's positive orientation in the face of adversity. There is solid research to indicate that positive emotions and positive outlook are infectious amongst group members, especially the impact of the leader. Developing the positivity of one's own leadership character is a powerful resource for being able to enable teams to function in the face of setbacks and continual tough demands.

Implications of positive social psychology on leadership.

Research in positive social psychology has identified four key capacities that triangulate to create a powerful capacity of the individual to function under demanding and stressful conditions. Importantly, when a leader demonstrates these four capacities, there occurs a significant and beneficial impact on the emotional well-being and functioning of the team. The four capacities are: hope, self-efficacy, resiliency and optimism. The synergistic effect of these four capacities is known as positive psychological capital. These capacities are trainable and once developed will have immediate impact of the positivity of one's leadership character.

Hope: A positive emotional state based on a sense of being to achieve goals and an understanding of viable options and ways of overcoming obstacles.

Efficacy: The individual's belief in his or her ability to mobilize motivation, experience, skills and knowledge to achieve a course of action in a given context.

Resiliency: The capacity to bounce back from adversity, failure, conflict as well as the capacity to take on the increasing demands and responsibilities of leadership.

Optimism: An outlook that attributes positive outcomes to personal and group strengths, and negative events to temporary or situation specific causes.

Together these four behavioral attributes result in a more integrated and systematic approach to leadership and viable courses of action. A positive leader is also more conducive to proactively responding to the needs of followers and for developing more balanced approaches for handling followers. The popular notion of heroic leadership is a double-edged sword; it can have a negative connotation when founded on ego and self-interest.

A new leadership HERO is one that conquers self and not others.

In Shackleton's case the hero is a leader who serves and leads in the interests of all his crew even the naysayers who have the potential to undermine his leadership ability. He represents an example of how positive psychological capital is evident in character development to subsume ego and self-interest and engage and persuade followers using positive HERO traits of: Hope, Efficacy, Resilience and Optimism manifest in leadership character that exudes confidence and builds trust.

Responsible Leadership. Putting it all together.

Character is manifest in the leadership state of mind. It projects itself in ethos, interactions, tasks and relationships. It builds integrity and trust with followers. It inspires followership. It is the inner-essence of being an authentic human being and exemplary leader.

Leadership principles are as old as ancient history. The ancient Greek philosopher, Aristotle, provides wisdom that relates to the principles in his work on rhetoric and dialectic. This work could be termed a grammar of motives that influence leader-follower relationships. The leader needs intelligence, logic, dialectic and rhetoric to influence decision-making. The leader needs to understand that rhetoric is the art of persuasion and dialectic is the art of argument. One of the key indicators of a successful leader is the art of communication to influence and persuade followers. Aristotle identified that persuasion is developed in three approaches. He termed these three approaches to persuasion as ethos, pathos, and logos.

Ethos embodies credible persuasion. Leadership with character is trustworthy and has authority and is worthy of respect. Authority must be earned. This clearly differs from authoritarian, which seeks to demand or impose respect. Ethos that is credible is often conveyed through the leadership tone and style of communication that has ethical appeal. The exemplary leader Mahatma Gandhi exhibited this ethos.

Pathos embodies emotional persuasion. Exemplary leadership provides examples of the importance of emotional connection to enhance communication, dialogue and argument. It is an appeal to the common experience. It invokes a shared sense of suffering or challenge to create the emotional call to action. Pathos is evident clearly in the language behavior and actions of the exemplary leader Martin Luther King Jr.

Logos embodies logical persuasion. The leader must be skilled in deductive and inductive reasoning. In context the leader must be able to back up persuasive intent with the clarity of the claims, logical planning, statistics and logical evidence to build trust. Logos is evident in the exemplary leadership of Ernest Shackleton.

Working Wisdom to Know How and Know Why.

Every leader who has experienced difficult choices and setback has gone through personal soul searching. Knowing yourself, your context and understanding how to persuade followers that share the same sense of mission is critical to success. The wisdom required for leadership competency existed long before CEOs and management gurus drank from the same font. Aristotle differentiated between three different forms of knowledge that is required to self-master leadership. These three factors are: 'episteme,' 'techne' and 'phronesis.' Different professions embrace these forms of knowledge to varying degrees. Knowledge in turn shapes the worldview and can create clarity or myopia that make it difficult for collaboration.

Episteme: refers to knowledge that is abstract, generalizable and theoretical. It is a scientific knowledge, which can be explicit and validated about what is known.

Techne: alludes to technical expertise which is often expressed through quantitative measures and rigid procedures that work.

Phronesis: is experience that helps to actualize individuality, identity and aspiration as in changes for the betterment of society.

It is in the realm of phronesis and integration of ancient wisdom and great narratives that leadership education can be inspired, ignited, nourished and cultivated to foster and feed the heart, mind and spirit to lead and to serve. Responsible leadership thinking is action oriented based on know-how and know-why. It is leadership with purpose. It is not rational deterministic thinking about simply managing things. It is founded on insight and intelligence to inspire a vision, sense of mission and strategic direction. Much has been written on the concept of vision, mission and strategy and its importance to leadership. These concepts can be taught. However, applying them is not a simple concept. As with all "states of mind" caution is exercised to avoid a dogmatic or doctrinal mindset that disconnects or devalues those with different states of mind.

Leadership has intentions. It is action oriented. It seeks to influence, persuade and remind. It has remits, agendas, interests and opinions. It has bias in its communications. Leadership is like unpeeling the multi-layered onion.

Leadership is situated within overlapping layers of identity. The core is founded on identity such as ideological, cultural and professional. These layers shape values, beliefs, norms and motives. Professions have identity that is exhibited in ethos, beliefs and esoteric thinking and sense-making prisms that create meaning. They see things through a selective moral and sense making prism such as a war-fighting lens, an engineering lens, a sustainable development lens, and a policy implementation lens. The third layer is the individual identity. It is unique, complex and shaped by environment, experience and education. This three-dimensional model of identity is evident in the crisis context which sharpens the heart, mind and spirit reflexes.

Leadership identity in these contexts is under siege. The real stresses and uncertainties of conquest, capture or failure can switch the leadership state of mind to a survival mode and default identity that reverts to old thinking and old beliefs shaped in experience, myths and meaning. The default identity phenomenon is evident in professions, organizations and contexts of conquest, merger and acquisition. Leadership and identity are challenged and conflict in these contexts. Failure to engender a shared ethos at a deep level can result in transfer of allegiance when disaffected followers become the enemy within. The responsible leader is conscious of this fact and understands the need to build the trust and integrity of followers and stakeholders towards a shared objective.

Countervailing Values and the Conflict of US, WE and THEM

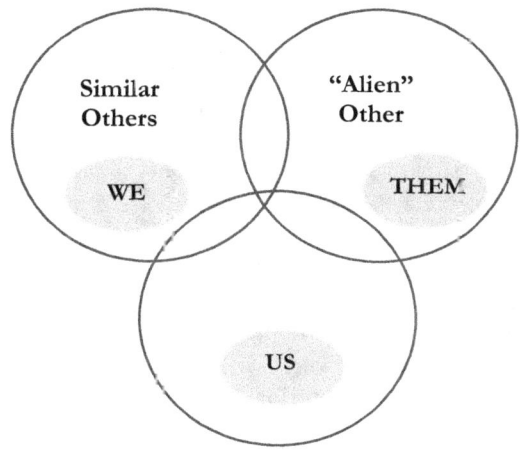

Figure 2: US, WE and THEM a moral prism focused on differences to frame and shape Conflict not Cooperation

Reference: Okros, Cultural Intelligence, 2008.

Chapter Summary

When we speak of the contemporary context of being uncertain, chaotic and crisis driven. We only need to look back through history to recognise that leadership, ego and hubris did not equitably serve followers and in many cases sowed the seeds for distrust and future chaos. Each era shapes unique contexts and challenges such as financial crisis, economic crisis and unstable states. The importance of leadership character is in nurturing the ethos that builds trust and integrity with followers and stakeholders to achieve the impossible.

Principled leadership character cultivates a listening heart, informed state of mind that aligns heart, mind and spirit.

It would seem that many individuals in organizations are without a shared mental map, or truly believe in or feel valued in a shared mental map. Leadership character can only be cultivated in a healthy culture or organization that values and validates heart, mind and spirit at all levels.

Contemporary teaching of leadership often draws on the cognitive constructs of the industrial paradigm. Instead, new mental models and organic living systems thinking are required to recognize that leadership in organizations is more akin to anatomical organisms where positive energy flows through arteries and creates healthy outcomes. In ancient Greece, where Western civilization was born, there was a recognition of the importance of these environmental influences. The main themes of Hippocratic medicine are health as a state of balance, the importance of the interdependence of the mind and body, nature's healing forces, ways of life and the various components of human nature, described in terms of "humors" and "passions". This Hippocratic understanding recognized the connection of heart, mind and spirit.

In today's organization stress is at endemic levels as a spirit to serve is absent. Leadership as a state of mind is anchored in the domain of character and ethos. Reflect on a context that you have experienced or know about that required leadership character and serving ethos to succeed. Reflection on lessons learned from both failure and success provide important lessons to inform future actions.

Shackleton's Leadership Challenge: Leadership with Character.

Shackleton's leadership character is grounded in his family motto: "By Endurance, We Conquer." He was raised with strong values of service in a loving family. He learned at an early age the need to serve and lead. This ethos served him well on his early voyages which tested his character and capability as a leader and follower. A leader like Shackleton prepares for a voyage satisfied that all is in order, but when all precautions fail to disclose unforeseen challenges and crisis it is obligatory to ride the storm.

Contemporary Leadership Challenge: Case study 'Character underpins ethos'.

Character is the nuclear core of responsible leadership. It energizes and radiates in the values, vision, motives, words, deeds and actions of the responsible leader. Working with professionals enrolled in leadership programs, it is easy to recognize the leadership ethos founded on good character traits. It is humbling to read candidate submissions to enter leadership programs. It can be seen in the values of parenting, volunteering, serving and leading in family, community and workplace. It is evident in young officer candidates who volunteer to serve their country and engender the values of "truth, duty, valour."

These core values vary depending on the institution but in essence they are grounded in the mantra: to serve and lead with integrity. A relevant example comes from the experience of one of the authors working with mentoring an MBA student who was completing an internship for a community organization. The meetings were held in the boardroom of a local hospital. One could experience the character of this institution not simply by the vision, values and mission on the wall. It was evident in the words and actions of the staff in living these values. The author asked his elderly father a decorated veteran who had served throughout World War II of what leadership character did he consider an exemplary leader should possess so that the troops would follow anywhere. He responded with a few well-chosen words. "From my experience the leader must support his troops.

He must be trusted. He must have courage. He must project moral authority for others to willingly follow." These character traits are the anchors that enable responsible leadership to be resilient and have the strength to do the right thing. To start to change the market behaviour resulting from toxic leadership, business schools need to ensure ethics and service are an integral part of the core curriculum.

Leadership Log – Principle 3: Leadership Character

Understanding Character in informing, guiding and shaping thoughts and deeds.

> - *Character provides direction to the state of mind.*
> - *Character fosters emotional connection to lead.*
> - *Character anchors competency and capability to lead.*
> - *Character projects authentic commitment.*
> - *Character and serving ethos foster trust and integrity.*
> - *Character is leadership doing the right thing.*
> - *Character is courageous and resilient in action.*

Self-reflection for self-mastery on leadership character.

Make notes in your *Leadership Log* to help self-master leadership in context. Answer the following questions as they apply to leadership character in your work context:

How does your leadership manifest itself in a serving ethos to connect followers to achieve the mission or objectives?

Reflect on the values that you have exemplified in your actions. How did you explain your reasons for the actions you took? How do colleagues get to see your leadership character?

How do your leadership competencies align with the organizational mission?

> *How do you know you had leadership agency in an important interaction with others?*
>
> *How well do your leadership values and behaviors align?*
>
> *How well have you been able to influence others in a responsible manner?*

Understanding principled leadership and multiple intelligences are foundational for the development of the responsible leadership mind which aligns heart, mind and spirit. It is not just a cerebral quality. It is a living anatomy that pumps energy and ignites followers to reshape contexts.

You have now completed chapter three and the third principle of leadership. Take time to reflect on Shackleton's leadership journey so far. Take a bearing on your own leadership journey - where you started from, where you are at and where you want to be in the future. What does it tell you about how you have experienced and handled tame, wicked and crisis contexts?

Leadership is not all about plain sailing and fair weather. The principled leader stays the course and learns valuable lessons from success and failure. They fall seven times and stand eight. It is seeing things through to conclusion that matters. At this juncture take a bearing on what resonates with you and what needs to be improved and or deleted to move to principled leadership in action.

Shackleton's leadership character is grounded in his family motto:

"Fortitudine Vincimus." - "By Endurance, We Conquer."

A leader like Shackleton prepares for a voyage satisfied that all is in order, but when all precautions fail to disclose unforeseen challenges and crisis it is obligatory to ride the storm.

Chapter 4 Leadership Confidence
Moral Purpose, Moral Authority
TRUST BUILDING TRAITS AND FOLLOWERSHIP

Shackleton's voyage to the Southern Ocean is a world of Roaring Fifties - fifty-foot waves, fifty-knot winds, icebergs and whales.
Painting by the author of Orca killer whales.
Confident authority and stealth to patrol their domain in the Southern Ocean.

"Life to me is the greatest of all games.
The danger lies in treating it as a trivial game,
a game in which the rules don't matter much.
The rules matter a great deal.
The game has to be played fairly or it is no game at all.
And even to win the game is not the chief end.
The chief end is to win it honorably and splendidly."
                                        Ernest Shackleton

THE FOURTH PRINCIPLE – LEADERSHIP CONFIDENCE WITH MORAL AUTHORITY

"Because one believes in oneself, one doesn't try to convince others. Because one is content with oneself, one doesn't need others' approval. Because one accepts oneself, the whole world accepts him or her." - Lao Tzu

"As soon as you trust yourself, you will know how to live." - Johann Wolfgang von Goethe, Faust: First Part

"Believe you can and you're halfway there." - Theodore Roosevelt

The lived voice of responsible leadership on confidence. Jean Vanier on being human: "One of the marvelous things about community is that it enables us to welcome and help people in a way we couldn't as individuals. When we pool our strength and share the work and responsibility, we can welcome many people, even those in deep distress, and perhaps help them find self-confidence and inner healing."
— Jean Vanier, Community And Growth

Leadership confidence is about followers having faith in the leader and feeling that they can rely on that leader. The leader needs to be able to engender a sense of trust with followers and to be able to create a sense of positivity around what they are attempting to put into action. The followers need to see the leader as confident, having moral authority and being able to relate to them as people. The leader needs to be on target in a fundamental way with the needs of followers and be able to create the feeling that "We have every confidence in their ability to succeed."

"Con-fid-ence" is by definition "to have faith."

Confidence is an essential requirement of the authentic trusted responsible leader. The more you project it, the more it grows. A lack of confidence is soon recognized by followers and leads to an erosion of trust and moral authority in the ability to effectively lead. It rapidly erodes the confidence of followers in supporting shared objectives. Confidence ensures followers have faith in the leader. The leader with ethical character and confidence is trusted. This results in a moral leadership that is secure in the ability to lead and differs in intent and outcome from insecure or toxic leadership, which is ego and hubris driven, and relies on fear or favor to attempt to gain follower engagement.

The effects of hubris and false confidence can be seen in examples of toxic leadership in the contemporary context where confidence tricksters deceive people after gaining their gaining their trust. The principle of confidence is the belief that followers have faith in the leader. A leader such as Shackleton projects resolute confidence in his self-assured belief in his ability to achieve extraordinary goals.

CHALLENGE 4 - LEADERSHIP CONFIDENCE TO BE RESOLUTE IN PURPOSE

Shackleton was faced with the dreadful realization that the expedition was trapped and essentially abandoned at the ends of the earth. There was no radio communication back to base, no one on the outside world knew what had happened, there was no rescue ship, and they were completely on their own. Shackleton's moral compass was pivotal to their survival. He had to provide the dead reckoning, the certitude around a course of action that would lead to their survival. Dead Reckoning is a nautical term, it is the estimation of the ship's place without any observation of the heavenly bodies. The distance run by the log measures it; the course steered by the compass, then rectified by allowance for current, leeway and ship's trim. Shackelton as leader uses his moral compass to take a personal dead reckoning on who he is, where he is, who he leads and what he stands for to have the moral authority to lead and build trust.

All leaders will have a dead reckoning when faced with a crisis context and wicked decision-making. The test of their leadership is in how they respond to crisis.

Confidence requires a disciplined mind to build trust, integrity and understanding when matters must be discussed in confidence for the common good. In working with professionals, it is evident that leadership theory can be taught but it requires a positive mental attitude and confident state of mind to apply principles in practice to be relevant. Confidence is an interesting word when understood by dissecting its original meaning.

Confidence derives from the Latin *confidere* to "have full trust."

The confidence of the leader engenders a sense of confidence in followers and shared sense of purpose and optimism. Confidence is evident in psychic pay-off in being part of a winning team or organizational culture that believes it is more than the sum of its parts. It requires transparency and authenticity to rebuild trust. It creates the opportunity to find a better way to develop ethical responsible leadership to sustain people and the world. To be clear, leaders are not the same as managers, chairpersons or facilitators. Leaders have conviction and personal ambitions. They must lead in organizations in which others sometimes disagree.

Imagine the stark reality of Shackleton's leadership confidence and ability

For ten months the ship and its crew drifted to the north until the enormous pressure exerted on the hull crushed it in and the vessel sank. As if this was not enough, the sinking of the Endurance initiated what must undoubtedly be one of the most remarkable stories of survival in history. For five months the whole ship's crew of twenty-eight drifted north on a huge ice floe - that shattered and shrank as time passed. No one could sleep and expect to wake safely in the morning. Shackleton displayed his superb leadership during this very trying period. The long period of relative inactivity on the ice floes demanded enormous patience from Shackleton but somehow, he held the group together, displaying caution when needed, and never permitting his firm control to slacken.

Consensus on one specific definition of leadership is unlikely or indeed impractical in the contemporary context. What is evident is Leadership is about doing the right thing.

Although Leadership involves a social contract, albeit implicit, it is not about popularity. It is about having the character and confidence to persuade people with egos and agendas to do the right thing.

Leadership is a social construct. It is embedded in culture, profession and identity. In a world that operates beyond cultural, professional and geographic borders it is time to re-examine and advance a responsible principled leadership ethos to reduce the trust deficit and develop approaches to engender a moral ethos that cultivates trust, integrity, service, stewardship, collaboration and sustainability. The responsible leader needs to understand the art of persuasion and influence focused on doing the right thing.

Imagine yourself as a leader in this changing and crisis context

In seven short days they had gone from a well-ordered existence on a sturdy ship to become castaways in one of the most savage regions of the world. They were drifting they knew not where, without hope of rescue, subsisting only so long as Providence provided transient sea life as food to eat. In these crisis conditions in the evening light the banjo would be played for a sing along and others would read aloud each night. Underlying the optimism and good spirits of the party was a deep-seated confidence that their situation was only temporary.

A crisis context heightens the individual strengths, weaknesses and traits of the crew. Some of the crew were difficult, others trying and others willing to help. Shackleton paid special attention to the characteristics of each crew member and adapted his behaviour to ensure that each of them was assigned tasks that would involve them in building a willing coalition working together for survival.

Leadership with character and confidence is trustworthy and has moral authority and is worthy of respect. Authority must be earned. This clearly differs from authoritarian, which seeks to demand or impose respect. This is often conveyed through the leadership tone and style of communication that has ethical appeal. It is evident in the leadership of Gandhi who exhibited a serving ethos focused on doing the right thing. Exemplary leadership provides examples of the importance of emotional connection to enhance communication, dialogue and constructive argument. It is an appeal to the common experience. It invokes a shared sense of suffering or a focus on success through a call to action. Leaders with a shared sense of collective responsibility have been able to empathise with suffering to make a call for principled action. Martin Luther King Jr., the civil rights leader, in his famous speech in 1963 outside the Lincoln memorial in Washington, enabled the support of the nation and galvanized his followers to act.

> *Now is the time to make real the promises of democracy. Now is the time to rise from the dark and desolate valley of segregation to the sunlit path of racial justice. Now is the time to lift our nation from the quick sands of racial injustice to the solid rock of brotherhood. Now is the time to make justice a reality for all of God's children.*

The leader must be confident and resolute when faced with crisis

Resiliency involves both handling the daily hardships and courage to take on risks and challenges, and the ability to bounce back from difficulties and disappointments.

Moral authority to lead is the precept of behavior founded on the tenants of religion or philosophy. Ethics is the accepted standard of that behavior. Confidence is undermined when these are not clear or deemed negotiable to achieve objectives.

The leadership prism for interpreting this moral spectrum is to understand the role ethics and values at play in leader-follower interactions. They are manifest in a sense of fair play, a fair-go for all, treating others with respect, living by the golden rule of treating others as you would wish to be treated. Ethos and values are evident in a corporate credo, religious creed and military esprit de corps. For the responsible leader to act ethically and be socially responsible differs in interpretation in cultures and professions. This reality is a mind-field in contexts that are in conflict, fractured or broken and where it is difficult to predict outcomes or end game goals.

Responsible leadership is doing things right that must be done

Shackleton was aware of the potential stress and trauma to his crew and realized they had abandoned ship and moved on to the pack ice. They had lost a context of security and they needed reassurance. He was hands-on in attending to this change in context. He recognized that the stress would drain the crew physically and mentally. To ensure fairness all crew were assigned and required to do any task they were asked to do. This was not without contention as a ship's crew had signed on for specific work as outlined in orders to mariners that applied only on the ship.

With great foresight he had thought through potential challenges and had the crew sign a contract prior to sailing to ensure his authority would continue until the end of the expedition no matter what the context. The crew would also be paid until the end of the expedition. This contract was reread to the crew to swiftly stop any silent sabotage to the mission's success. Even in this crisis context Shackleton recognized the importance of symbolism, ritual and celebrating important occasions to build a cohesive crew with a sense of esprit de corps. The three ship's boats were renamed after key sponsors and the ship's carpenter a skilled, experienced mariner set to work to strengthen the boats ready for the arduous open sea journey across the ice with the objective of reaching the open sea and the glimmer of hope of being rescued. In these arduous contexts the leader and crew are faced with their own mortality.

It is in these crucial moments that the responsible leader has a personal epiphany to trust in heart, mind and body to lead others. This rare type of wisdom relevant to practical action implies good judgement and character in habits or practical virtue. It is illustrated in Thoreau's classic narrative when reflecting on being in the moment in the simple act of *Walking:*

> *"I have met with but one or two people in the course of my life who understood the art of Walking, that is, of taking walks, - who had a genius, so to speak, for sauntering: which is a beautifully derived "from idle people who roved about the country, in the Middle Ages, and asked charity, under pretense of going a la Sainte Terre," to the Holy Land...."* Thoreau, *Walking.*

Chapter Summary

The leadership deficit and time to check decline in confidence.

In the contemporary context a leadership deficit is evident in how toxic leadership has created, influenced or responded to social, economic, financial, political and environmental crises. In the contemporary context crises are often inter-connected across national and inter-organizational boundaries. The evidence is indisputable and the costs undeniable.

Leadership is fundamentally about helping humanity. The human population is growing exponentially and challenging living systems, scarce resources of the world and taxing existing mental models for developing responsible leadership approaches to these exigencies. Unfortunately, many individuals in organizations are increasingly *sauntering* in a landscape or with a mental map that they truly do not believe in or feel valued in. Responsible leadership with spirit can only be cultivated in a healthy culture or organization that values and validates heart, mind and spirit at all levels. Recognize that confidence building is a two-way process between leader and follower required to succeed.

Shackleton led from the center. He listened to his crew and to malcontents and won them over. The leadership principles of character and self-confidence are the foundation for developing the competency and capability to serve, lead and excel in any context. Confidence is to have faith in oneself. Often at the root of insecure leadership is lack of confidence and self-worth. This could have deep roots back to childhood, school and past negative experiences. It is important to recognize that we are all people of worth. Some individuals are privileged in having a secure past with positive experiences that strengthen self-worth and self-confidence. Others may have been impacted by factors that have weakened self-confidence and have reinforced the negative. These roots need pruning for fresh growth to become the whole person in mind, body and spirit and the confident leader they need to be. We are all people of worth. As Gandhi said we can be the change in the world. It is important to come to terms with past experiences that may impact our present self-confidence and limit our future potential. Shackleton's leadership confidence to build the trust of followers was achieved by some of the following:

> - Positive State of Mind, Heart and Sense of Optimism: Evident in his handling of the crisis situation and providing hope and direction to his crew.
>
> - Self-Confidence to Project True Moral Courage.
>
> - Evident in his leadership character and fortitude to endure to succeed
>
> - Trust in Self and Others to Succeed not Fail.
>
> - Evident in his words, deeds and actions as a leader with principles and purpose.
>
> - Trust in Faith, Hope and Providence to prevail.
>
> - Evident in his inner character (exhibiting moral purpose and moral authority).
>
> - Evident in his alignment of principles and sense of purpose that never wavered.

The leadership principles of character and self-confidence are the foundation for developing the competency and capability to serve, lead and excel in any context (that is, the enactment of the 7Cs).

Shackleton's Leadership Challenge: Leadership confidence.

Shackleton would face hardships that almost defy belief, and it was his ironclad resilience that allowed he and his men to survive. The story of the expedition is the story of surging optimism met with crushing defeat manifested over and over and over again. That the former never failed Shackleton, and the latter never broke him, is truly what brought his men through to the other side.

Numerous times, Shackleton and his men felt incredibly hopeful that a goal was in sight and things were turning their way, only to have these hopes utterly dashed. This is a time when moral authority and moral compass keep the leader on task. It is about the confidence in measuring one's moral ability to lead.

Contemporary Leadership Challenge: Case study the importance of self-confidence

Working with highly talented individuals in leadership programs, a common trait that is evident is an assured sense of self-confidence and determination to succeed. This trait is evident in speaking, deportment and interactions with others. It is evident in submissions that provide clear positive mindset that see challenge as opportunity to influence and shape outcomes. Sometimes the listener observes that confidence can cover for other traits where the words don't always reflect the actions. Confidence at its root is to have faith in one's actions. the leader with moral character and strategic capability is able to project confidence and this in turn creates confidence in his or her team. A leader lacking confidence is a liability to themselves and followers. They project uncertainty and indecision which in turn erodes confidence with a team. Confidence and positive outlook are the bedrock of the leadership state of mind required to succeed.

Leadership Log – Principle 4: Leadership Confidence.

Understanding Confidence founded on moral authority to serve and lead others.

> - *Moral purpose in leadership is essential for the confidence to do the right thing.*
> - *Confidence is founded on moral authority required to trust in their leader.*
> - *Confidence of the leader creates trust in followership a shared sense of purpose.*
> - *Confidence enables the leader to subjugate ego, hubris and hidden agendas to do the right thing by his followers.*
> - *Confidence underpins self-reverence, self-awareness and self-worth.*

Reflection for self-mastery of strengthening leadership self-confidence.

Step 1: Reflect on the confidence you have in your ability and determination to follow positive leadership paths to succeed.

Step 2: Release negative toxic thoughts as they weaken our mind, body, spirit and ability to serve and lead. Focus on positive affirmations.

Step 3: Radiate gratitude and a grateful heart to be your true self and find true north and become all you can be as a person, as a leader and lead with self-confidence.

Step 4: Focus with a resilient mind on your personal vision, mission and objective.

Step 5: Commit to serve and lead others with the confidence to succeed together.

"And the elements' rage, the fiend-voices that rave, Shall dwindle, shall blend...O thou soul of my soul! I shall clasp thee again, And with God be the rest!"

Browning.

Chapter 5: Leadership Courage

Uncommon Strength and Resilience to Lead with Purpose
COURAGE, TRIBULATION, ENDURANCE, HOPE

Shackleton and a volunteer crew launch the ship's boat on the courageous 850 mile Antarctic open sea rescue mission. This dangerous trip has never been successfully achieved since.
Painting by author based on surviving photographic plates.

"Optimism is true moral courage."

"Fortitudine Vincimus - By Endurance We conquer."

Shackleton quote and Family Motto.

THE FIFTH PRINCIPLE – LEADERSHIP COURAGE TO FACE ADVERSITY

"Being deeply loved by someone gives you strength, while loving someone deeply gives you courage."
— Lao Tzu

"Success is not final, failure is not fatal: it is the courage to continue that counts." — Winston S. Churchill

"I learned that courage was not the absence of fear, but the triumph over it. The brave man is not he who does not feel afraid, but he who conquers that fear." — Nelson Mandela

The lived voice of responsible leadership on courage. Robert Merton, a sociologist, drew attention to the phenomena of how purposive social action can lead to unintended consequences. Leaders might at times benefit from serendipitous unintended consequences but more likely will have to counter criticism and rebuke for unwanted or unexpected consequences of actions they have pursued. In any event leaders need to have the courage to persevere in the face of adverse unexpected consequences. The principle of leadership courage refers to the capacity of the leader to demonstrate uncommon acts of valor and strength in the face of personal pain, grief, adversity and death. The leader can draw on inner strength (character) to tackle the big problems, deal with the untidy stuff that is confusing everyone, and to lead by example. Courage and self-sacrifice, however, are uncommon virtues.

In the case of Shackleton, the Antarctic explorer Sir Vivian Fuchs thinks that Shackleton's change of plan probably saved them from disaster if they had attempted the original objective. At the time though, the mood was grim as Shackleton had to pull out all stops to devise a new plan of action and carry the crew with him. This was a time when all hands-on deck were needed, and personal courage was required to move from disaster and despondency to determination and dedication to the task at hand. This was a life and death context. In these conditions a leader comes face to face with gruesome decisions to be made. He ordered that all the dogs were to be shot. This is no easy task as the crew had become emotionally attached to the sledge dogs by name. It had to be done. The dogs were shot and eaten by the crew. Rarely is a leader faced with these hard decisions that must be made. We do not know our own leadership courage and capability to lead others so that they will follow until we go through the crucible of leadership in extreme contexts of life and death.

CHALLENGE 5 - LEADERSHIP COURAGE IN DOING THE RIGHT THING

The principle of leadership courage refers to the capacity of the leader to demonstrate strength in the face of pain, grief and adversity. The leader can draw on inner strength (character) to tackle the big problems, deal with the untidy stuff that is confusing everyone, and to lead by example to pursue worthwhile purpose. The leader enacts courage by leading with Heart, Mind and Spirit. The foundation for this leadership is integrating a clear sense of what is right (ethos), feeling the need of others (pathos) and understanding what can be achieved (logos). In the real world, leadership is a messy affair. There are no clear-cut actions and outcomes. Followers can be difficult, sponsors can be political, organizations can be toxic and psychopathic, and any action can trigger unexpected and unwanted consequences.

Shackleton had the inner strength and courage to face the hard stuff and the soft stuff to be resolute in leading in adversity. Imagine the crisis unfolding and the responsible leadership and courage required to simply stay focussed on survival.

The order to abandon ship was given at 5 pm. For most of the men, however, no order was needed because by then everybody knew that the ship was done and that it was time to give up trying to save her. There was no show of fear or even apprehension. They had fought unceasingly for three days and they had lost. They accepted their defeat almost apathetically. They were simply too tired to care. On one trip to the stricken ship a group of men ran the red, white and blue Union flag up to the forward yardarm, the only rigging still standing. When the Endurance went, she would at least go with her colours flying. They watched in silence. Away across the pack ice. The stern of the Endurance rose 20 feet into the air and hung there for a moment with her motionless propeller and damaged rudder, then slowly, silently, she disappeared beneath the ice, leaving only a small gap of open water, which then closed. It had all happened in ten minutes.

Shackleton noted that night in his diary that the Endurance was gone and added: "I cannot write about it." A ship is a physical symbol, a tangible reality that linked them to the outside world. She had carried them safely halfway around the globe. Now she was gone. There was nothing but endless ice. Their position was 68 38 and half South, 52 28 West. A place where no person had ever been before, nor could they conceive that any person would ever want to be again. Shackleton's order to abandon ship, while it signalled the beginning of the greatest of all Antarctic adventures, also sealed the fate of one of the most ambitious Antarctic expeditions. The goal of the expedition was to cross the Antarctic continent overland from west to east. Evidence of the scope of such an undertaking is the fact that after Shackleton's failure, the crossing of the continent remained untried for fully forty-three years.

The long days and nights ahead on the ice will require inner strength and resilience to lead with a sense of purpose focused on success. Shackleton occupied himself poring over every available chart to figure out the best routes. He planned how best to implement the survival plan to exploit it to the fullest including preparing equipment to succeed in the new context. This new context unsettled some of the crew and starts to lead to unrest among a few of the crew. Shackleton realised that this unrest could rapidly lead to sedition if left unchecked. He led by instinct to take on the naysayers and reread the signed contract made by each crewmember to remind them of their duty and obligation.
Shackleton had a higher vision. He would not let his crew die on the ice.

Shackleton displayed his superb leadership during this very trying period - keeping everyone busy, making preparations for any eventuality and maintaining morale. Outwardly his spirit of leadership never flagged, although his diary reveals his deep concern for the crew and their situation. The plan discussed with the crew was to march toward Paulette Island, 346 miles to the northwest, where the stores left earlier should still be. They would be dragging their two boats on sledges weighing more than a ton a piece. This would be across the ice, with its pressure ridges occasionally two stories high. Nevertheless, there was a remarkable absence of discouragement. They had no time to reflect on the terrible consequences of losing their ship. It was time to commit to the task at hand.

The journey commenced led by an advance party to guide the way. The teams came next, pulling sledges loaded with 900lbs apiece, the boats, drawn by fifteen men harnessed in traces. It was a killing toil because of the weight, the boats sank into the soft surface of the snow. The progress was slow and arduous and after three hours they were only one mile from the ship. Eventually after the super-human effort of hand pulling the boats across crevices and shifting ice floes, they reached the open sea.

On reaching the edge of the polar ice they launched the boats into open water. His determined resolution ensured that his crew of twenty-seven were ready to launch the boats as soon as the pack ice enabled an opening to sail across the open sea to the potential destination of Elephant Island...a desolate spot in Antarctic waters. The three ship's crews each were assigned a leader as they could soon be separated by the vagaries of wind and wave. They all knew their destination would be Elephant Island. This journey was estimated to be two days sailing across treacherous dangerous water in open boats surrounded by icebergs and pack ice. The task to make human contact for eventual rescue demanded discipline and order to keep everyone alive in freezing conditions.

The destination of Elephant Island would require an arduous voyage across the stormiest ocean in the world in boats, the largest being twenty-three-foot-long. They would need to sail to South Georgia, some eight hundred miles away. As was to be expected, Shackleton lead the rescue attempt himself with a tough crew of six with the goal of rescuing the others on Elephant Island. The journey would become a breath-taking journey of courage, skill and determination under the most demanding conditions. Taking overloaded boats through the ice, with seventeen hours of darkness in twenty-four hours across the polar sea in seven days constituted a truly remarkable feat of leadership. This context is one where courage, experience and skill come to the fore. These were hardened mariners skilled in the art of navigation and seamanship.

Constant communication of the sub-conscious mantra of "pull, pull, pull" was needed as every sinew and muscle pulled at the oars to keep the boats moving. Miraculously even though separated they all made it to Elephant Island. Huxley said of Shackleton's leadership when faced by the impossible he succeeded. He lived by the leadership mantra of: "find a way or make one." His indomitable spirit breathed life into his followers who believed in their leader.

While this survival journey was unfolding another narrative was unseen and in play. At this stage Shackleton has not been seen of or heard of for some time. It would be easy to write him and his crew off in a context where a world war was losing thousands of lives every day. Here is a time where Shackleton's wife plays a major role in keeping the story alive and the public interest and sponsors on the radar. Here we see the importance of working together and understanding that the outer political context shapes the future of the present crisis context. It was important to understand the political reality of decision-makers who can influence and support or deny a relief mission. The key players are The Royal Geographical Society, Government, Media and Sponsors. With World War I unfolding, lay Antarctic explorers are not seen as a priority. As is expected government stalls for time and sets up a relief committee but stalls and does not immediately take action. In this context Lady Shackleton works with the media and sponsors to keep the spotlight on the expedition and the urgent need for a relief expedition while weather conditions make it possible.

Shackleton has the inner strength and courage to face the hard stuff of survival and deal with the soft stuff of morale and wellbeing. To be resolute in serving and leading in adversity to ensure the wellbeing and resilience of the crew.

Courage is not a word used lightly. It is an uncommon quality

To lead and have others follow in this Antarctic context takes a certain leadership character. The explorers Scott and Shackleton provide comparative examples of two leaders who both had courage, similar objectives but with a different leadership character. However, **Scott a courageous leader who died in his attempt to reach the pole is less remembered for his leadership**. Robert Falcon Scott was a Royal Navy Captain through and through and in an age of sail he was the Captain who ruled and expected discipline and obedience. Shackleton differed from Scott. He had sailed with Scott on earlier voyages. Shackleton was a Merchant Mariner. His confidence came from his anchored character as leader and strategic thinker in non-traditional manner. He personally hired his crew. Shackelton broke down traditional hierarchies to build esprit de corps. He used one-on-one discussion to build trust. He put down dissent by sharing tents with malcontents. His leadership behavior was fair and caring for the period.

It is a fine line behind success and failure. Leadership lessons learned are that history can treat leadership legacy harshly. Truth is selective. Amundsen the Norwegian had rushed to the South Pole, eclipsed Scott, and captured the prize. Scott and crew tragically died in Antarctica. It is said that Scott's story and tragic death were read at the time across the British Empire and installed a stoic ethos that was manifest in the hardships and courage of those in the trenches.

Although Shackleton failed to meet his objective, he is remembered for his leadership confidence in always telling his crew that they would all survive, He would not let them down and indeed he kept his word. Scott is less remembered for his scientific findings, which were substantial. He had continued to drag heavy samples of rocks on his sledge rather than abandon them.

Shackleton's expedition was a failure. He lost his ship and failed on his mission. Yet he is remembered as a great leader for saving all of his twenty-seven-member crew from certain death. His leadership character and courage emerged to be tested in the face of crisis. Trapped in the Antarctic ice with his ship crushed. He exhibits the leadership character that inspires hope and engenders fortitude amongst his crew.

The painting at the start of the chapter portrays one of these acts of heroic courage. It is based on the surviving photographic plates that were dragged by man hauled sledge across the polar ice to ensure that a record exists of the survival experience of the Endurance crew. We see how leadership character, confidence and courage are essential traits of the exemplary leader in inspiring followership. This is evident in the action of the leader and crew to continue to work and function together after living for ten months on the ice in a final attempt to survive. The role of leadership courage in this crisis context is responsible for maintaining a healthy, mind, body and spirit both as leader and followers to sustain motivation and reduce stress and anxiety of the crew that could create despondency and sink the mission.

While he did not complete the Antarctic journey he had hoped for, he brought back all twenty-seven of his crew alive, an example of exemplary leadership character and courage.

The Australian explorer Douglas Mawson survived similar hardships that inspired further generations in research and discovery of Antarctica. The prize may not be the original goal. The surviving of a crisis requires sustaining resilient leadership to achieve an uncommon objective that most deemed impossible. Crisis is the leadership crucible. It is the testing ground where leadership, character and courage are forged or fail. Having the leadership state of mind and personal courage that can adapt to crisis and reshape the mission in this context is evidence of exemplary self-mastery to lead others. After ten months on the ice and man hauling, by sledge, the ship's boats were converted into sturdy sailing vessels to attempt the dangerous rescue operation. This is one of the greatest recorded feats in history of a small boat voyage in horrendous open Antarctic weather. Shackleton and a small volunteer crew sailed 850 miles to South Georgia Island. An unprecedented open sea voyage and one of leadership, courage, fortitude and endurance. This is courage in action. The responsible leader in this context has to make hard choices in tough situations. What is required is the personal courage to carry on and lead by example. Signs of weakness will weaken resolve. To paraphrase Shackleton's language said in his time:

> "If you're a leader, a person that others look to,
>
> you've got to keep going."

Face to face leadership in tough situations requires the leader to emotionally connect with the group. Doing so takes courage as the leader exposes his or her personal self to the group sense of identity and their emotional demands. This connection occurs at a deep human and authentic level. It is not about listing politically correct statements. Rather the leader needs to identify what is troubling the group, understand their fears and state the values and norms that will enable the group to flourish. Social identity theory identifies the deep human resources that the leader needs to draw on are conviction, passion and courage. Conviction means that the leader has understood the context sufficiently to know what to commit to, passion is the capacity to connect to followers at both an emotional and cognitive level, and courage is the capacity to pursue what is right.

Leadership is most sought after in times of uncertainty and confusion, when people are distressed and fearful and the old routines are no longer working, and change is needed to adapt to new circumstances. At these times people are also at their most vulnerable and will respond to attractive visions and overly confident leaders who promise easy solutions. These leaders often are motivated by hubris and lack real understanding of how to adapt to changing situations. In contrast, what is really needed in these situations is the leader with courage, who has the tenacity to work through the difficult problems. These responsible leaders have a sense of moral purpose and are able to persevere with engaging people in putting in the sacrifice to work towards worthwhile goals. The leadership principle of courage is a rare quality. It requires the leader to be prepared for self-sacrifice and valor in the face of personal danger or the threat of harm. Courage is manifest from inner personal strength that overcomes fear to act in the face of danger, pain or grief.

Leadership requires the courage to deal with the tough problems and work with the people to bring them along in a purposeful change process.

> "The leader who stays "safely" in the realm of the veiled and the sheltered, who stays on the known paths, is unlikely to lead others to new ideas, to new territory or towards a new vision...It takes courage to leap and it takes wisdom to reside in the new-found territory of thinking where everything is different". (quote from Elizabeth Smythe and Andrew Norton, in their 2007 article *Thinking as Leadership/Leadership as Thinking*).

Leaders need courage to act when things are unclear as well as being able to tackle the unexpected courses of action. They need to resist the mounting social pressures of a crew who need to see leadership courage in action to lead by example. Leaders who demonstrate courage have a powerful impact on followers. Foremost, followers believe and trust leaders who show courage since they know they can rely and count on these leaders in the face of setbacks or threats. Next, followers are inspired by courageous leaders to lift their own game and live up to their own values and to stick with goals when the going gets difficult. Importantly, leaders who display moral courage in a transparent manner lift the whole ethical tenor of the group or organization. At the outset, Shackleton made no bones about the mission and the requirement of those that served with him. His newspaper advertisement used for recruitment says it all:

> *'Men wanted for Dangerous Expedition: Low Wages for Long Hours of Arduous Labour under Brutal Conditions; Months of Continual Darkness and Extreme Cold; Great Risk to Life and Limb from Disease, Accidents and Other Hazards; Small Chance of fame in Case of Success."*

It followed that those recruited fit the mold and this served them well when disaster struck, and all hands-on deck were required to man the pumps and save all possible supplies to survive ten months on the ice. It is an essential quality of the responsible leader who serves and leads from inner personal strength, to be able to tackle the big problems, the untidy stuff, to pursue purpose, and lead by example. Contexts can be uncertain without clear outcomes. The law of unintended consequences shows how a leader must have the courage to reshape the context to succeed in adversity.

Walking the walk and talking the talk ensures that there is no "SAY-DO" gap between what was said and what was expected

Recognizing our current understanding of leadership and the need to advance the enlightened leadership ethos requires being courageous and taking bold moves. Shackleton's epic Antarctic voyage of survival story provides leadership lessons and teachable moments that provide examples to mentor approaches back in the workplace.

The education of the leader is life-long and the introduction to the great leadership narratives and lived stories is a process that helps foster a love of learning and inquiry. This integrative learning process leads to greater reflection to foster the ability to reshape contexts and provide leaders and followers with hope. These personal qualities are required to succeed in collaboration and cooperation. Reviewing the narratives of great leaders who exhibit spirit and presence is an inspiring and uplifting experience. The exemplars are individuals who had the vision and the spirit to envision a broken world anew. They uplifted the spirits of others and by force of character and presence achieved the impossible. As Jonathon Swift, a 16th century satirist and cleric, and author of Gulliver's Travels, said: "vision is the art of seeing things invisible." Turning vision into reality is the task of exceptional leadership.

A recurring narrative in the contemporary leadership context has been that the world has become increasingly complex, chaotic, compressed and crisis driven. This narrative is under-pinned by a deeper human crisis of confidence in trusting the ideology, values and mental models that previously had helped shaped a more stable industrial era paradigm and world view. These mental models are increasingly perceived as obsolete, dysfunctional and perhaps even harmful. The emergent paradigm towards an inter-connected, information and social networked world is crossing old boundaries and creating a mind space where countervailing ideologies, values and intention meet. This emergent reality requires a shared vision with the ability for reflection and the moral perspective to make decisions that inform the leader-follower narrative with a responsible leadership ethos that underpin collective action. Potentially this space is where the leader's spirit and presence can bring together hearts, minds and spirit to collectively make sense of ethical dilemmas shaped by an amorphous moral prism.

Chapter Summary

Leadership role models needed for the courage to lead in a contemporary context being shaped by crisis and change.

Old mental models of leadership are characterised by legacy knowledge and value systems of command and control, often based on stereotyped assumptions of leadership from the military and industrial era. These old mental models can continue to influence thinking in the leadership industry as it shapes a desired identity, ideology and intentions to compete and win. These mental models can be valid in command and control situations. However, they do not provide the leadership thinking, behavior and approaches required to tackle the messy and often wicked problems of an inter-dependent world driven by crises. The old mental models of power, command, control and conquest help foster approaches that lead to We, Them and Us. It is a world focused on highlighting differences not similarities. This mental model is seen by critics as a worldview of competition, conflict and conquest of winners and losers.

Paradigms do not simply shift from one way to the other way of learning. We are at a leadership crossroads where we have the opportunity to educate both men and women to take us to a better more equitable future that is sustainable through good stewardship and principled leadership. This approach integrates the masculine and feminine strengths and is focused on collaboration and compromise for the greater good. Or we can continue down the same path that has resulted in increasingly short-term toxic ego-driven leadership, which has rewarded unethical practices and the success of a few and the suffering of many.

Leadership mindsets, ethos, courage, consensus, collaboration.

People do not change without a reason. It often takes pain and suffering to lead to recognition, redemption and rebirth. We see this in recent living memory in the context of World War II and the ultimate defeat of Germany, Italy and Japan which lead to untold death, destruction and suffering. It is a dangerous path to follow the wrong leader who leads a nation over the edge. Out of the ashes of this suffering like a phoenix the rebirth of new thinking and enlightened leadership emerged. It was fortunate that in the end the winning powers were swayed by the leadership of US Secretary of State George C. Marshall to rebuild and not punish these nations.

The recent conflict in Afghanistan, which has lasted longer than World War II, has required a collaborative leadership process of defense, diplomacy and development working together to fight the war and find ways for peace and reconstruction. Achieving these outcomes is asking a great deal from anyone in leadership in any organization. It requires a special kind of leader who can work within the culture and at the same time be an agent for change. It will take personal courage, sacrifice and resilience. At the end of the day it will be a personal legacy of a life of leadership with integrity and accountability. Like Shackleton, we have a choice. We can focus on hope, optimism, resolve and endurance to succeed. Each of us can be the new heroic leader focused on conquering self not others. We can become a role model of responsible leadership. Like that grain of sand in the oyster individually and collectively working together for good we can be the change in the world. The question is do we know ourselves and do we have the courage to travel down a path less travelled that has its own rewards. Like Shackleton's leadership journey this is not a sprint but rather a marathon that leaves a legacy.

Shackleton's Leadership Challenge: Leadership Courage

Using a small ship's boat Shackleton and a selected crew made one of the most courageous open ocean voyages in history to seek help and rescue all the crew left behind. This experience produced an archetypal heroic responsible leader far more than the attainment of his original intended goal would have done. Shackleton was clearly a leader who had courageous qualities, and he galvanized his followers to follow him literally to the ends of the earth and back.

Contemporary Leadership Challenge: Case study leadership courage

In the British Commonwealth, the Victoria Cross (VC) is the highest award for valor and courage in the face of personal danger. To be award the medal is recognition of exceptional valor and courage exhibited by an individual. Visiting the Australian War Museum, one passes through a long open walkway where on the side wall there are bronze panels on which are inscribed the names of Australia's war dead, listed under their unit designation. It is a deeply moving experience that recognizes the individual valor and courage of those that served and made the ultimate sacrifice. It is quiet and dignified with a sense of gravitas. Inside is the tomb of the unknown soldier and in the museum are listed those that have been awarded the VC and their own story. It is truly humbling and sobering. It is a place of silent reflection and veneration. It makes one aware of our mortality and own legacy. Each nation has similar edifices to those that have died in the service of their country. What would these heroes have to say to the present generation of leaders about service and sacrifice? To serve, to lead and to be responsible as a leader would have been expected.

Walking along the harbour side in Toronto there is a monument to the firefighters who lost their lives in doing their duty. A busy throng walks by mostly oblivious to the monument. Yet without their sacrifice the city would surely burn. One ponders on how a corporate monument would celebrate courage in doing the right thing. What would it say about leadership and legacy? Recently the obituary of a local business leader was in the paper. This leader had grown up poor. He had made a fortune and his great joy was to open summer camps for underprivileged kids to experience better things. He had the courage to live his life, he had served his country, he had been a cop and he went on to build an iconic business that enriched and gave back to the community. It takes courage to create your own authentic principled leadership path. It takes a different courage than laying down one's life. As a leader we have been given authority and obligation to serve others. We have inherited the blood, sweat and tears of those that came before.

Now is the time to have the courage to meet the contemporary challenges of a world in need of responsible leadership.

Leader Log – Principle 5: Leadership Courage

- Leaders who demonstrate self sacrifice and valor.
- Leaders who work from the front and centre.
- The courage to do the right thing at the right time.
- The courage to walk the talk.
- The courage to be decisive for the greater good.
- Courage provides the determination to lead with purpose
- Courage enables the leader to tackle the hard problems and handle the messy stuff.
- The courage to ultimately sacrifice self to save others.

Self-assessment for understanding leadership with the courage to face real adversity.

Courage is what happens in the moment. It can be an act of great valor. It can be the courage to suffer for the greater good. It takes many forms. We will not know about our own courage until we come face to face in the moment with a life and death moment or in the workplace of speaking truth to power unafraid of the cost and consequences.

Reflect in your leadership log on Shackleton's lessons learned in understanding courage. This reflection is like a mirror being held up to look into your inner self.

Chapter 6: Leadership Commitment

Communication, Connection and Collaboration
COMMIT, COMMUNICATE, CONNECT

Endangered Blue Whale diving in the Southern Ocean.
Largest mammal on the planet able to communicate across vast distances.
Painting by the author who crewed in the Southern Ocean.

"We had seen God in His splendors, heard the text that Nature renders. We had reached the naked soul of man."
                                                                Ernest Shackleton.

THE SIXTH PRINCIPLE – SUSTAIN LEADERSHIP COMMITMENT TO OTHERS

> "Desire is the key to motivation, but it's determination and commitment to an unrelenting pursuit of your goal - a commitment to excellence - that will enable you to attain the success you seek." - Mario Andretti

> "Unless commitment is made, there are only promises and hopes; but no plans." - Peter F. Drucker

The lived voice of responsible leadership on commitment. One outstanding senior police officer comes to mind as an example of commitment. He was a person who inspired his subordinates. He walked the walk and talked the talk. The police force is an institution that is uniformed and hierarchal. It takes a champion with commitment to be the leader who can change the culture. This senior officer led by example. Not only did he have his officers take the graduate leadership program but he also took the program and studied with same cohort for two years together. This example demonstrates how leadership commitment creates understanding and develops engaged followership by connecting and collectively committing to create change.

The leadership principle of commitment means dedication to a cause or activity. It is a promise to commit to do something. It is a covenant based on trust between the leader and follower to engage in a duty that restricts freedom of action.

The principle of leadership commitment is about followers believing in the leader and with the shared goals of leader and follower. The leader builds commitment through words, deeds and the daily practice of responsible leadership. The leader has a keen focus on important and worthwhile issues and the trust developed amongst followers means that they see the leader as someone who is worth following. The leader's dedication to service and duty is crucial to the building of trust amongst followers.

Commitment provides the linkages between the leader, the followers and the mission. Commitment flows both ways, between leader and follower, as well as commitment to striving towards worthwhile outcomes. Key aspects of Shackleton's leadership are his commitment to his crew, his ability to connect with his crew and lead from the center, his ability to communicate by talking the talk and walking the walk.

The leader has a keen focus on important and worthwhile issues and the trust developed amongst followers means that they see the leader as someone who is worth following. The leader's dedication to service and duty is crucial to the building of trust amongst followers. Commitment provides the linkages between the leader, the followers and the mission. Commitment flows both ways, between leader and follower, as well as commitment to striving towards worthwhile outcomes. The task of the leader is to shape the interpersonal and social environment to support followers to connect and to commit themselves to supporting the leader, group and the mission or goals of the group. The research on social identity theory provides important insights into how groups form, stick together and function.

Foremost in the context of groups and teams, the individual becomes more influenced by a sense of shared group membership, that is the social self that is defined by "we" rather than a personal self that is defined by "I". Furthermore, the group members identify with a set of shared norms, values and goals and share motivation to work collaboratively to pursue the interests of the group. Group members respond positively to a leader who can focus on the qualities of the group and can explain why they are special in some important way. The leader becomes the advocate of the group identity and actively needs to promulgate the unique identity of the group. This identity in turn needs to reflect the important values and norms of the group. An effective leader is tuned to the values and emotions of the group members and understands what is important when addressing the group or in responding intuitively to crises as they occur.

The principle of leadership commitment requires followers to believe and trust in the leader's ability to succeed together.

Doctor Philip Law, a former Director of Australia's Antarctica Divisions wrote in the 1980s: "Nothing is so important as the appointment of a first-class leader and nowhere are the qualities of leadership subjected to more grueling tests than at an Antarctic station. One quality is fundamentally essential to any team. It is loyalty. A man must be loyal to the expedition, loyal to the leader and loyal to himself. Some men are naturally loyal; some are fundamentally antagonistic, critically outspoken and disloyal". Knowing this, it would seem sensible for a leader, in choosing his team, to seek out naturally loyal individuals rather than knowingly to lay up trouble for himself or herself by taking self-avowed critics. The responsible leader understands and respects loyalty and provides a pathway for loyal followers to commit to a worthwhile cause or endeavour.

Internal to the group, the key behaviors of the leader include a care and concern for followers, an emphasis on strengthening relational ties with group members, respecting the human dignity of group members, and acknowledging their value to the group, and demonstrating how the group can impact on the external environment in a way that provides the group with positive outcomes.

Shackleton was committed to his crew. This had been earned and was trusted. His followers then had commitment to succeed.

CHALLENGE 6 –LEADERSHIP COMMITMENT TO SUCCEED AS A TEAM

We have followed Shackleton since he headed south in the Endurance into the Weddell Sea. Initially they had cleared the pack ice on January 9 but by October the ship had become trapped and was abandoned on October 27 and eventually sank on the 21st. of November The loss of the ship was indeed a crisis as they had to reorganise stores and equipment, and camp on the polar ice and move quickly to new camps as the ice continuously broke around them. Finally, by great fortitude, determination and commitment they crossed the solid pack ice by dragging the heavy-laden ship's boats on improvised sledges. They had to live for months in extreme conditions on the ice and Shackleton kept a close eye on making sure that they rested and had hot food and rest before moving on. They eventually reached loose pack ice, and in April of the following year they launched the boats and sailed into the frigid open sea to Elephant Island an uninhabited way station. Key aspects of Shackleton's leadership are his commitment to his crew, his ability to connect with his crew and lead from the center, his ability to communicate by walking the talk.

These attributes of the leader make good sense aboard a ship travelling into hostile waters and the unknown. They make good sense in an organizational context. Every team member must know their duty. They know that commitment has consequences. They either sink or swim together. Failure to meet these commitments can have severe consequences.

Consider the modern Antarctic leader and crew who access global satellite communications and are connected 24/7 back to a support base. They have helicopter support and the latest equipment onboard for all eventualities. Even so disaster can quickly strike with the failure of pumps and equipment can sink a more modern version of Endurance. The leadership commitment and capability of highly qualified followers are the pivotal component required to avert disaster.

It is worth considering the lessons that could be learned in the contemporary context in how the financial crisis could have been avoided if captains of the financial industry lived by a similar leadership code of conduct and commitment. Commitment and capability determine how effective the leader has been in understanding the context, demonstrating the character required to lead the group and building the confidence and trust of followers. In having the courage to communicate honestly what the group must face to achieve success or avoid failure if possible. Commitment requires connection between people at a human and authentic level.

Back on Elephant Island Shackleton selects six volunteers to join him in the strongest ship's boat the newly named James Caird for a truly heroic dash across 850 miles of open arctic water.

The goal was to reach South Georgia and the Norwegian whaling station, civilization and a base to re-launch a rescue attempt to retrieve the remaining crew. Shackleton wisely leaves the two ship's doctors behind to take care of the remaining crew members. The crew are suffering badly from frostbite, with some requiring amputation of toes without anaesthetics. He appoints a second in command to ensure leadership is in place in his absence and informs them of instruction should he fail to return. The two remaining boats are upturned to make storm proof shelters for survival. Their diet is seal and penguin. The crew had previously learned that they could eat dog but not dog's liver, as they were full of enough mercury to poison a person. Even in these drastic conditions, morale was high, and the crew would sing at night to comfort themselves and have discussions to distract the mind from the harsh reality.

On April 11 the James Caird is launched and the rest of the crew wave them off as they head out into the open sea. What follows is surely one of the most heroic open water crossings in history. Travelling through fifty-foot waves and fifty-knot winds and taking navigational sightings the James Caird reaches South Georgia on May 10. It is said that the crew arrived more dead than alive. But alive they were. They had achieved the miraculous. Shackleton later referred to the third man phenomenon and spoke of an additional person that he felt had followed him on his survival journey and offered them support. Shackleton attributed this feeling to his strong faith. They had made it. They then realized that they had arrived at the opposite end of the island to the whaling station. There was only one thing stopping them: a mountain and its glacier. The crew rested and managed to snare a young Albatross in the nest, which gave them the nourishment to survive.

The next stage of the journey would require the three of them to attempt to climb the mountain and cross the glacier. None had any experience in mountaineering. Not to be deterred, they roped together and started out. They were to succeed together or die together. Trust and focus on real issues mean that this leader is worth following. The crew believes in the leader. Commitment is the ability to energise the nexus between leader, follower and mission.

Back in London, the government had finally decided to set up a relief committee with only eight weeks window before the ice closed again. It is probably best that Shackleton had no knowledge of the slow progress being made on his behalf.

Developing leadership commitment is an investment that pays dividends. It is an investment in human capital that grows exponentially on the initial installment. It is a trust account. It is leadership currency that funds and sustains a better future and a better world. The currency of leadership is part of the new vocabulary and language of leadership required to change the existing narrative of leadership that feeds the deficit.

Commitment from a responsible leadership perspective is to "talk the talk and walk the walk." Commitment is ensuring there are no "say-do" gaps between what is said and what is done. Consider the consequences of "say-do" gaps evident in a corporate vision, mission and implementation strategy. These potential gaps can lead to increasing cynicism and disengagement across an organization and among stakeholders that do not trust the words, the actions and in turn the promise of a brand. Commitment requires that the leader clearly communicates objectives and connects with followers at an emotional level.

The Practice of Responsible Leadership.

Responsible leadership is a worthy calling. It is a life-long pursuit. It is not simply an intellectual pursuit. It requires heart, mind and spirit to engender a serving ethos in life, in profession, community, nation and vocation. It is a reflective mindset, enlightened ethos and strategic leadership ability that creates and exudes confidence and positive energy in words, acts and deeds for transformation. It has a lofty dream and strategic vision of responsible leadership for sustaining people and creating a better world. Leadership and humanity are at an ethical and environmental crossroads. The need for taking the path less travelled to cultivate responsible leadership, talent, ethos, harmony and purpose is an ethical imperative. Responsible leadership is a pursuit of the human spirit. It creates the serving leadership ethos that provides hope and opportunity. The reward is in creating a legacy of doing the right thing, work well done, people and communities respected, nurtured and sustained.

In practice, responsible leadership involves facing some obvious fundamental challenges: motivating followers; mobilizing their knowledge, skills, and abilities; creating and implementing an organizational vision; and managing change. Competing ideologies and lack of trust are mental barriers that require deeper understanding of how professional identity and integration of stakeholders works in practice.

In the contemporary context we are as tribes, nations, institutions and individuals rowing not always together in one ship in need of repair to keep afloat on one blue planet. Some leaders may still not recognize this fact. Others are in denial looking at mental maps that are cartographic fallacies, designed to manage and measure recollections that do not fit the new territory. It is time to roll-up this old mental map. Some leaders are profiting, many followers are stymied, or others suffering in an unhealthy toxic environment and have signs of dis-ease. Rewarding toxic leadership of "titanic" acts of hubris, ego-gratification, self-interest, and self-preservation has moral and ethical consequences. The acts erode trust, loyalty, commitment and impact behavior of followers and stakeholders. Responsible principled leadership is becoming the defining issue of our time. The ethical imperative for moral leadership is required to build trust, integrity and confidence.

The exemplary principled leader has managed to lead and balance profit and principles. They are not required to do this. It is a state of mind, an ethos. It makes good sense to invest in people and communities. This trajectory is founded on the golden rule of do unto others, as you would have them do unto you. The currency of responsible leadership is an investment that keeps growing. It creates momentum, it changes lives, it enriches the future, and it supports a sustainable and hopeful future. Leadership and Commitment is the opposite world-view of Machiavelli's *The Prince* of self-interest of what most governments do but none profess to do, and the tough realities of developing leadership currency in messy organizations and the wicked problems of the world.

We arrive at a place where we began. Know Thyself. The evidence suggests that principled leadership creates hope and opportunity. It unleashes talent and potential for people and a better world. The present leadership deficit created by toxic and unethical leadership is devaluing the very currency of leadership. Responsible leadership is the real reserve currency If invested wisely it addresses the issues of inequity, poverty, peace, development and sustainability.

Reflect on your leadership commitment. Take away the trappings. To paraphrase Shakespeare: "what more is a king than mortal man except the ceremony that surrounds him." Now, what is your leadership currency? What is its real worth? Does it entail selling your principles? This seems to be evident in toxic leadership currency. It is this state of mind that is behind the leadership deficit and economic deficit that hurts people and communities. It will always be there. It has been well mentored and well rewarded.

Responsible principled leadership's reward is in a life lived with purpose and principle worthy of the human spirit. It is urgently needed to avoid abdicating accountability and leaving millions to take the path to poverty, inequity and conflict that come back as retribution. The media tends to cover the unethical leadership dilemma as it sells papers. Good news is hard to find in the world of social media. It is evident clearly everywhere and at every level. The world is full of unsung heroes and willing followers hungry for ethical principled leadership in the workplace and community ready to invest in the real currency of leadership.

Lessons about Commitment and Capability Gaps in Crisis Contexts provide a sobering reality check.

In our research on leadership in crisis contexts, we found that common themes emerged from leaders at all levels across public, private and NGO sectors. The locales of leadership were often fractured, blurred and poorly defined with no clear end point. These included: Afghanistan and the SARS health crisis as cases in point. Leadership professionals involved in these crisis contexts worked in diverse organizations engaged in policing, security, defense, health, financial, institutional, service and NGO sectors. The professions and ideologies differed. The leadership challenges in the context were often seen differently depending on perspective to the needs. The SARS health crisis, Tsunami relief and Afghanistan deployments required developing leadership capacity to create collaborative approaches to work in locales where identity, ideology, values, mindsets and perspectives where often barriers to success.

Evidence of the Urgent Need for Principled Leadership.

- Banking and Finance Sector – Lack of Confidence, Trust Erosion.

- Economic Sector: Governance and Corporate Social Responsibility.

- Health Sector: Pandemics, Food Safety, Surge Capacity needed.

- Fragile States: Instability, Poverty, Conflict, Terrorism, Chaos.

- Fractured Communities: Human Security and Sustainability gaps.

- Public Sector: Whole of Government leadership capacity gaps.

- Planet Stressors: Climate, Environment, Migration, Starvation.

- People Dying –Poverty, Pandemics, Conflict in 24 Nations (Defined by UNHCR as lack of food, health, equity in political process, participation in wealth generation and sustainable wellbeing of people).

- Profits not equitable: Inequity and injustice. For those in power or in denial, the global economic crisis is seen as a minor crisis in comparison to climate, environmental, pandemic and migration issues.

Mental Barriers to an enlightened leadership ethos include:

- Economic optimists making decisions in urban enclaves that are disconnected from the context of indigenous and collective wisdom.

- Institutional learning is departmentalized by professional cultures and elites with diverse motives, mandates and intents that require managing tensions for possible collaboration.

- Collective wisdom of indigenous peoples is detached from decision-making.

- There is a lack of approaches for interdisciplinary collaborative learning/praxis.

- An ethical moral philosophy is not fully developed to create a sharing community, which is essential to leadership, governance, human rights and trade justice.

- An absence of engaged future leaders forming cohesive social networks and learning communities

- A deficit of integrative mental models to foster common wealth and common space.

In these contexts, the field research identified areas that need to be addressed to strengthen leadership capacity. Non-cognitive intelligence in the form of collaboration is required to make sense of context, issues, ideologies and the crisis terrain. In interviewing post-deployment personnel who had served in crisis contexts, a common recurrent theme is the need for developing the leadership mindset required in deployment and on returning from the harsh reality of crisis to enter back into the society and organization. Field research in these contexts identified that competency, training and skills were at a high level. However, in need of strengthening were tacit learning to prepare leaders to lead where the theatre, actors, scripts and narratives made sense-making and decision-making difficult. The mental map did not often fit the actual territory.

In the past, leaders were prepared for the challenges of leadership by ritual, religion, and literature, which helped prepare them for harsh contexts. Increasingly men and women of diverse belief, culture and backgrounds work together. This requires further development of the psychological, cultural and spiritual aspects of leadership to create common ground.

The Prototypical Leader: Rethinking Leadership.

The roots of leadership are bound in mutual respect, obligation and mutual survival. Leadership plays a pivotal role in human development. It has deep roots that go back to our ancient collective ancestors living in groups and tribes for security and survival. The global crises challenges leaders to reflect on moral sentiments that recognize that leadership is a sacred trust not simply the pursuit of power. This leadership perspective would suggest a values shift towards a:

- Dialogue not War. Recognition that this is an unconquerable world.

- Leadership collaboration based on trust, integrity and sacrifice.

- Social, economic, environmental, sustainability stewardship.

Defining capital more broadly than simply financial capital should include human capital EQ (emotional intelligence), intellectual capital IQ (institutional intelligence) and strategic intelligence SQ (strategic intelligence). Developing a strategic understanding of these three forms of capital leads to a new way of perceiving and measuring what matters beyond the traditional bottom line and ROI Return on Investment. Measuring EQ, IQ and SQ requires developing a triple bottom line and measuring EQ (return on integrity), IQ (return on intelligence), SQ (return on investment). This redefinition of the concept of capital leads to revisiting the enlightened era thinking at the birth of the modern world and the inquiry into the wealth of nations and moral sentiments that underpin stewardship of wealth and well-being.

There is a growing community of educated leaders in public, private and NGO sectors across national domains that are engaged in ethical leadership and emergent strategies to better inform policy and sustainable decision-making. It is worth reflecting that the word "crisis" in the Chinese language represents both danger and opportunity and viewing crisis as an opportunity helps to re-assess the broader issue of how training and knowledge transfer could be developed to solve many of the existing problems requiring leadership capability.

Chapter Summary

Commitment connects the leader, follower and mission success. The building blocks for an enlightened leadership ethos are trust, integrity, humility and courage in adversity. Without a shared code of conduct, the concept of vision and mission statements to guide leadership and followership norms and behavior are simply words on a wall and not accountable to the action that takes place in the halls. The ability to communicate is an essential requirement of a leader to build commitment and requires understanding the role of ethos, logos and pathos to persuade, influence and inform stakeholders of issues, actions and consequences. Leading in the contemporary context can be overwhelming as individuals seek to try to balance life, work and other obligations. We need to be resilient and remain optimistic and have hope in the present to reshape the future context. We do not need prophets of doom but prophets of hope.

Shackleton's Leadership Challenge: leading with the commitment to succeed.

Responsible leaders like Shackleton make a commitment to reshape contexts leading by example. Incremental change is often more resilient and sustainable than attempting an objective that is so lofty that we fail to attain the goal. The future context will not be a level playing field. It will require stealth and guile of the leader who seeks to chart a better future founded on core values of a serving ethos. As Martin Luther King Jr once said: "Let us realize the arc of the moral universe is long, but it bends towards justice." We need to dare to dream to imagine a better future and turn this into reality one day at a time. Shackleton understood the power of words and power of positive thinking to inspire the commitment of followers. How we chose to think and act to build commitment and to shift the leadership narrative to principles with purpose is up to us.

Contemporary Leadership Challenge: Case study leadership commitment:

The toxic leadership that created the financial crisis has undermined our trust, loyalty and commitment to institutions. It has now manifest in the rise of populism in politics by those that feel left behind or ignored. It will not go away any time soon. The behaviour and role models of responsible leadership need to be told to counter the cacophony of negative role models. Trust, loyalty and commitment may have been undermined but in the hearts of many, goodwill to others still exudes. An example of this is the SARS health crisis that unleashed a crisis in the health and wellbeing of communities. In this case the SARS crisis rapidly crossed borders from Asia to North America.

In Toronto, Canada's largest city, it took hold. Toronto is a multicultural city with a large Asian community. Suddenly crisis hit and hospitals were overwhelmed, restaurants became empty and wearing masks became the new norm. Universities, the home to international students, had to develop contingency plans to respond to this unfolding crisis. Suddenly a vibrant international metropolis is challenged by a health crisis that does not respect place, power or privilege. This epidemic posed a leadership challenge where commitment was required. Leadership can arise from across an institution or community. Health care workers were now in the front line they were committed, courageous and capable. They fought to bring this health crisis under control. They lacked the surge capacity. They needed a collaborative approach. They needed communications that calmed and informed. Through the dedicated efforts the crisis was checked. It took the lives of front-line health professionals and patients. Loyalty and commitment to serve others saved the day. The response of front-line health professionals illustrates an exceptional example of responsible leadership. It begs the question of how different the response was by those in leadership positions during the financial meltdown where many were rewarded with bonuses for their toxic leadership. Both these examples provide learning opportunities in MBA programs of what leadership founded on a serving ethos could look like in practice.

Leadership Log – Principle 6: Commitment.

- Commitment is founded on trust between the leader and follower.
- Commitment is built on shared dialogue and shared purpose.
- Commitment mobilises followers that are engaged at a deeper level to succeed.
- Commitment connects the leader and followers with the vision, mission and strategy.
- Commitment is earned not bought and can easily be lost when trust erodes.
- Commitment creates esprit de corps and sense of belonging to a shared cause.
- Commitment is the link pin between the leader and follower to sustain resilient capability focussed on success not failure.

In your leadership log reflect on how your leadership style could strengthen follower commitment to achieve shared objectives. Does this self-reflection suggest possible areas to work on in serving and leading others?

Chapter 7: Leadership Capability
Responsibility, Results and Return On Investment

RESPONSIBILITY, RESPONSIVENESS, RESULTS

Shackleton illustrated his exceptional leadership capability here, in his crisis context to focus on mobilizing and leveraging leadership capability to survive and succeed.

Above painting by the author based on observation of frozen terrain.

> "*Difficulties are just things to overcome, after all.*"
> "*Superhuman effort isn't worth a damn unless it achieves results.*"
>
> Ernest Shackleton.

THE SEVENTH PRINCIPLE – LEVERAGING LEADERSHIP CAPABILITY

"Man often becomes what he believes himself to be. If I keep on saying to myself that I cannot do a certain thing, it is possible that I may end by really becoming incapable of doing it. On the contrary, if I have the belief that I can do it, I shall surely acquire the capacity to do it even if I may not have it at the beginning." - *Mahatma Gandhi*

"And when we think we lead we are most led." - *Byron*

The lived voice of responsible leadership on capability.
Working with the serving professions provided a real-life locale to implement Shackleton's seven responsible leadership principles in action. This included mentoring firefighters and health care professionals who then led teams to facilitate the Shackelton leadership exercise within their organizations. This mentoring process resulted in energizing the respective teams around a shared narrative to evaluate their own strengths and identify opportunities for change and areas to leverage leadership capability to respond to challenging and crisis scenarios.

The facilitation process created a culture change for retention to advance the benefits of responsible leadership. Importantly it created internal champions committed to lead and to serve.

Leadership capability refers to the capacity for purposeful change and to be able to engage followers to achieve outcomes. Leadership capability is where the rubber hits the road. It is about responsibility, responsiveness and results. Leadership capability is the capacity to take intention and turn it into reality through the efforts and commitment of followers. Leadership capability requires a leader who has developed his or her capability to an extent where they can connect with followers in an authentic and purposeful way to sustain and achieve objectives. These concepts and relationships have been well studied in the leadership research especially in studies on transformational leadership.

However rather than try to integrate volumes of research and theory, we have provided a practical approach integrating the seven principles that are grounded in lived experience. The 7Cs of leadership is based on solid theory and research, but this is in the background and the focus is on what you can do as the leader to achieve your capability. The actual capability to succeed will be impacted upon by environmental factors.

As Shackleton states: "That when things are easy, I hate it."

CHALLENGE 7 – MOBILIZING LEADERSHIP COMMITMENT TO ACHIEVE THE SEEMINGLY IMPOSSIBLE

Although Shackleton had to abandon the original mission of reaching the South Pole, he achieved a remarkable feat as a leader by constructing a new plan of action in the face of crisis, motivating his crew to follow him, and in bringing all expedition members back to safety and in in good mental spirits. A key outcome of leadership that is often overlooked is the cost of the leader's ambitions on the followers' health and wellbeing.

Highly instrumental leaders can treat followers like machine parts to be replaced when they suffer fatigue and become mentally and physically exhausted. An important role of the leader is to maintain the well-being and resilience of the followers, since it is this human potential that provides the ongoing capability to achieve outcomes.

Shackleton's commitment to his crew was total. He suffered when they suffered. He expected no special treatment. He walked the talk with each of his crew no matter what rank or background. Eventually by sheer determination, luck and providence the three eventually wandered into the Norwegian whaling station They had achieved the impossible. Shackleton wasted no time to attempt a rescue mission to retrieve his entire crew before the ice froze. He made four separate attempts before succeeding. He did not step ashore because the ice was starting to turn. On August 30, on the fifth attempt, four months and six days after leaving in the James Caird he rescued his entire crew.

Within three months, most of his crew had volunteered to serve at the front in a world war that seems to have no end.

The contemporary context is also one of inter-connected crises, competition, corruption, chaos and complexity. It is unstable and constantly changing. It is a mind-field. It requires of the leader exploration and navigation through uncharted territory. The contemporary context shaped by complexity and crises is one of messy organizations, wicked problems, asymmetry, short-term thinking and mental models that were designed for the industrial stable context that underpinned leadership in organizations. In the new territory leadership founded on hubris will become its nemesis. Responsible leadership respects the reality that in the new contemporary context "we work together or whither together." It has a lofty dream and strategic vision of responsible leadership for sustaining people and creating a better world. Leadership and humanity are at an ethical and environmental crossroads.

People in the world, given the opportunity, still have the power to create a culture of responsible leadership and create a better future. Today we are in a crisis context and the future is uncertain. The secret is turning the shared vision of hope and opportunity into a new reality to inspire the human spirit with a sense of hope and opportunity. The integration of values and purpose can make principled leadership steadfast in a time of change. The word vision derives from the ancient Hebrew word for breath – *ruah*. It is not a vision statement on a wall. It is a spirit that transforms and breathes life into the organization. The secret is turning this new vision of leadership into reality and this requires responsible leadership capability and an action plan to succeed.

Chapter Summary

Leadership Capability Challenges to Embrace.

The leadership context has always been challenging for each generation. Shackleton worked in extreme contexts in uncharted lands. He comes from a long line of leaders who have pushed the margins of the known world. In the earlier age of enlightenment navigators such as Captain Cook had the leadership capability to travel to uncharted territory and chart the way forward for future generations. Cook's ship Endeavour was the namesake of the present-day NASA space exploration mission named Endeavour. Shackleton's, Cook's and NASA's missions are a continuous legacy that seek to develop the leadership mindset, advance competence and leverage capability to explore, research and discover emergent approaches that benefit people and the world.

In the contemporary context, with its emphasis on breathtaking technological innovations and social change, leaders can forget these historical precedents. They attend the same schools, listen to the same troubadours and ignore or are ignorant of the collective wisdom of the ages. It is time to reclaim and advance a responsible principled leadership ethos to reduce the trust deficit and develop empowering approaches to engender a moral purpose and enlightened ethos that cultivates trust, integrity, service, stewardship, collaboration and sustainability.

What is evident is that leadership is about doing the right thing.

Leadership is a social construct founded on shared meaning and shared engagement. Leadership is not a new topic. It has always been an integral part of the human condition for survival and protection. In this context a leadership deficit is evident in how recent leadership has created, influenced or responded to social, economic, financial, political environmental crises. In the contemporary context, crises are often inter-connected across national and inter-organizational boundaries. The evidence is indisputable and the costs undeniable. Responsible leadership is fundamentally about helping humanity.

The human population is growing exponentially and challenging living systems, taxing scarce resources of the world and overwhelming existing mental models of leadership for responding to these exigencies. The crisis context poses moral and ethical challenges for leadership in organization. It creates the opportunity to find a better way to develop ethical responsible leadership to sustain people and communities.

The root cause of crisis is a lack of responsible leadership and associated ethical failure. The experience in many contemporary contexts is one of leadership that has lost its moral compass and discarded ethical anchors. With neither compass nor anchor, the captains of these institutions have sailed wildly into uncharted waters and wrecked cargoes, careers and crews on the rocks of unbridled ambition. Unethical, toxic or weak leadership thinking and behavior in these institutions and organizations has created a breach of trust and betrayed followership. The unethical leader has abandoned ship as the 'seven seas' (7Cs) deluge to swamp ego and sink hubris. However, often not before these leaders use their positional power and influence to garner payments without responsibility for addressing the crisis. This new piracy is alive and well it has just taken on a different form. It is unfortunately still termed leadership.

Shackleton's Leadership Challenge: Leadership Capability

A less resilient and capable leader to Shackleton is likely to have been unable to gain the commitment of the group members and is likely to have faced death on the ice of the Antarctic. Shackleton is an iconic leader who had the courage to walk the talk and inspire a crew as a culture of leadership.

The responsible leader needs to be able to fulfill several roles to be really effective:

- Leader and Steward to lead and serve so others follow.

- Visionary and Strategist to provide the strategic direction.

- Navigator and Explorer to dare to lead a path less travelled.

- Captain and Champion to inspire super-human effort to excel.

Contemporary Leadership Challenge: Case study leadership capability

It is said that Michael Angelo made drawings for submarines and flying machines. Unfortunately, he was ahead of his time and did not have the capability to turn his vision into reality. One of the greatest landscape gardeners of all time was known as Capability Jones. Such was his reputation to turn wilderness into the epitome of the ordered English garden. Examples of leadership and capability are everywhere to be seen from Steve Jobs, Apple, Dysons, Vacuum and Whittles jet engine, Amazon and others. The sky seems to be the limit. Capability can be seen at the individual, team, organizational and national level. Tomorrow's China is already happening. Yesterday's customers are not today's consumers. Past successful empires and organizations that have failed to adapt have declined. In many experiences working with individuals in leadership development programs, the focus is nearly always on the individual. When these individuals enter organization, often they are frustrated because they feel that their skills are not recognized or required. Rarely discussed is the challenge of aligning leadership development to leverage organizational capability. Much effort is expended measuring the bottom-line financial metrics. Lacking is the same rigor in measuring the leadership metrics to succeed as an enterprise or organization. The seven principles of responsible leadership provide clearly identifiable indicators that leverage return on integrity, return on intelligence and return on investment.

In summary the seven principles relevant to the responsible leader in the contemporary context include:

1 Context. The contemporary context is laden with crises. In an inter-connected world, these are complex and multi-layered. This is a context where responsible principled leadership is urgently required and will be challenged and tested by those that have a vested interest in maintaining the status quo. It requires leaders with courage and fortitude. It requires character. It involves sacrifice. It requires rigor and resilience in implementation. The contemporary context is impacted by force fields of complexity, competition, chaos, crises, change, contradictions and conflict. These pounding waves of change challenge leadership thinking, behavior and strategic action in new territory.

Shackleton constantly studied the context and was able to adapt to changing conditions and the sinking of his ship. In crisis contexts he had the mental discipline to stay focussed on the end goal of survival.

2 Consciousnesses. We are at the leadership crossroads one road leads to the status quo and the other path less travelled is towards responsible leadership. In reading Shackleton's narrative and the 7Cs of responsible leadership, we seek and need to inspire a higher consciousness of responsible leadership and principled habits of the mind to embrace responsible leadership that is responsive and achieves results for the good of many and not just for the few.

Shackleton clearly knew himself. He knew his strengths and had a deep sense of self-reverence, self-knowledge and self-control that enabled him to stay focused and conscious of follower needs.

3 Character. Moral authority and moral purpose are founded on a character of integrity. What is not visible on the surface of a leader that informs their actions are the beliefs, ideology and learning that shape leadership character. This is the hidden side of leadership: what Carl Jung termed the shadow or collective unconscious. Just as the hidden part of the iceberg can sink an ocean liner, the shadow can engulf the unprepared leader. It underpins leadership character and capability. A firmly held leadership ethos is required to lead with principles and purpose.

Shackleton's leadership character as guided by his Ethos is evident in moral purpose to build trust in his leadership. Pathos his ability to persuade followers in an emotional manner to support the survival objectives. Logos his appeal to logic to clearly inform followers of the need to work together to succeed.

4 Confidence. Self-confidence requires having unshakable faith in one's belief, behavior and actions required to succeed. It starts to develop long before the individual becomes a leader in the workplace. It is initially cultivated at an early age of development by upbringing and schooling and is exhibited in work in family, community, church, school and volunteering in organizations. This is the fertile ground in which responsible leadership character is planted and shaped.

Shackleton's upbringing and personal knowledge of his chosen profession honed by experience resulted in confidence founded on faith and fortitude to ensure he did the right thing. His confidence helped to create a strong bond in his social contracts.

5 Courage. A rare quality of a leader is a willingness to sacrifice his or her interests for a belief, cause or to save others. This quality is formed often by the leader enduring a crucible experience in which he or she has had to look deep inside oneself. Learning from a crucible experience prepares one to lead without fear, favor or thought of the danger to self in the cause of service to country, self-sacrifice, defense in standing up to human wrongs and the undefendable in the cause of freedom and justice.

Shackleton's courage is evident in his personal capacity and strength of mind, body and spirit to endure hardship and danger to succeed at all costs. Failure was not an option. He lives by his family motto: "Fortitudine Vincimus – By endurance, We conquer."

6 Commitment. Is exhibited in leadership that commits to serve and lead with integrity to build trust and accountability in words, deeds and actions as an exemplary role model and mentor that followers will respect and support to create commitment to a shared purpose.

Shackleton's commitment was total in his dedication to the task. He saw it as a covenant between leader and follower to engage in a duty of service and leadership that guided his thoughts and actions.

7 Capability. Is the ability to turn a vision into reality. It is the ability to lead others in collective action in difficult changing contexts to sustain resilience and organizational competence and capability to reshape a context through leadership and mentoring to achieve exceptional outcomes.

Shackleton states: "That when things are easy, I hate it." He had the capability to be a visionary, navigator, explorer and servant-leader.

His personal capability inspired likeminded followers to collectively develop the strategic capability to succeed against impossible odds.

Shackleton exemplifies the seven principles of leadership in words, actions and deeds. He is an example of what responsible principled leadership can achieve.

Leadership Log – Principle 7: Leadership Capability in Action.

- Leadership Capability involves creating the vision, mission and strategy to excel and succeed.

- Leadership Capability is the ability to reshape the context and reinvent a better future

- Leadership Capability cultivates the ethos and distinct culture of purpose and performance.

- Leadership Capability engages the whole team of followers in pursuing purposeful change.

- Leadership Capability inspires followers to achieve what was thought to be impossible.

- Leadership Capability creates the resilient sustainable competency and capability to succeed.

- Leadership Capability embraces change and knowledge transfer to leverage organizational strategic capability.

Chapter 8: Responsible Leadership in Action
Responsible Leadership in Changing Contexts

NAVIGATING A RESPONSIBLE WAY TO SERVE AND LEAD

A small ships boat heads out into the uncharted sea guided by the stars a chart, compass and a responsible leader. On this journey there will be stiff winds, pounding waves, calm, squalls, storms, challenges and crew fatigue. When bad weather arises, it is essential that the sails are well set to ride the storm. This is a place where the responsible leader must navigate the 7Cs and lead the crew to succeed.
Above painting by the author

Through Endurance, we conquer

Ernest Shackleton.

RESPONSIBLE LEADERSHIP IN ACTION

NAVIGATING THE 7Cs TO SERVE AND LEAD

Throughout history responsible leaders have emerged to shape events. Sometimes these events have been real or fabricated, such as in a crisis, challenging or chaos situations, to engage people and mobilize communities to change and succeed.

1. Responsible Leadership Challenges in Context – Beware of Icebergs

We are living in a world experiencing multiple crises. There are threats to human security, energy security and the sustainability of the ecosphere. Ongoing conflicts devastate the prosperity of countries, traumatise communities and cause mass migrations of people into tenuous conditions. We are experiencing changes to the climate that will have major consequences for the future. Potential threats include rising water levels, crop failure, migration, disease, conflict, social-political and economic consequences. This future will create a new map of consequences and new leadership challenges akin to Shackleton's crisis context. Our leaders will require self-awareness, super-intelligence and responsible action. Today we see multiple crisis contexts that interact with one another and exacerbate the potential for disasters. The world has come to a crossroads in many areas, where responsible leadership is needed to steer us towards a better course ahead.

Leadership in the contemporary territory is similar to Shackleton's experience of trying to navigate across the shifting and cracking polar ice. The contemporary territory is being shaped by external stressors: of globalization, information fragmentation, time compression, demographic change, information fragmentation and government seen as cure-all in response to crises that are often inter-connected. The stressors are not unlike the global tectonic plates that shift, meet to create friction and build pressure on leadership and organizations.

Understanding the context requires perspective and insight to make sense of leading in a changing environment. The stressors have the ability to undermine leadership, organization and operations There are many cases in history where there has been a massive shift in the environment, perhaps due to new technologies (e.g. digitalization), or the entry of global competitors, where the organization becomes literally frozen in the ice of the old context and leadership thinking is unable to envisage the new emerging mental map.

Leaders are most valued in times of uncertainty, fear, dislocation and discontinuity.

The test of a leader is in being able to read the context and envisage a new way of doing business and engaging followers. The art of leadership is learnt through personal experience; as distinct from the detached theory of leadership, which is outlined in management textbooks. The crisis context poses ethical challenges for leadership in organizations. It will require transparency and authenticity to rebuild trust. It creates the opportunity to find a better way to develop responsible leadership to sustain people and communities. To be clear, leaders are not the same as managers, chairpersons or facilitators. They are individuals with the courage to serve and lead others in the pursuit of worthy goals that benefit all stakeholders.

Where leaders use hubris and acquisition to secure resources, power and influence the inequity gaps will grow. This type of leadership mindset is not and never has been a sustainable response for serving and leading responsibly.

Refer to Chapter 1 Leadership Log Self-assessment in understanding the context.

Make notes in your log to navigate and lead effectively in the contemporary context.

2. Responsible Leadership Consciousness – Ethical Perspective to do the right thing

Mental models simply do not disappear. Rather they morph or follow the laws of entropy and die a slow death. The personal qualities of future leaders will require both emotional and cognitive intelligence domains that underpin emerging leadership competency of collaboration and cooperation. Since the September 11 attacks in the United States (9/11), we have become more aware of the complexity of the conflicts within and between countries, as well as communities that cross state borders, and how states can be fractured along ideological fault lines.

The principled responsible leader is bound by a code of conduct, service and sacrifice. The ethical leader is archetypally the antibody that restores a diseased society that is suffering from hubris and toxicity. The principled leader acts to defend, strengthen and protect the organizational body politic from danger and disease. As a growing culture of leadership, they have the existential power to mobilize people and sustain communities. It is time to cultivate a culture of responsible principled leadership. Leadership is not about one individual in an organization. It is about a shared ethos throughout an organizational culture that shapes leadership thinking, behavior and intention at all. A consciousness is emerging created in part by globalization, interconnectedness, demographic shifts and increased awareness of the human impact on ecosystems.

Assess the relevance of old thinking paradigms engendered in legacy systems.

The human potential to secure a better future is limited by legacy systems, ideology and belief systems that reinforce myth and meaning of where we have come from, not where we have the potential to grow. Cultivating leadership requires developing new talent with leadership capacity to create the change. Urgently required is a responsible leadership ethos with the perspective to understand root causes and to identify collaborative approaches to build bridges of hope to respond to opportunities for sustaining peace and prosperity for all. It requires a recalibration of the moral prism to focus on hope and engagement.

Refer to Chapter 2 Leadership Log Self-assessment in understanding the state of mind.

Make notes in your log to navigate and lead by example in the contemporary context.

3. Responsible Leadership Character – Ethos, Pathos, Logos to Serve and Lead

The evidence from the field suggests the need for a responsible leadership framework that connects thinking hemispheres to support reflective informed decision-making for fostering trust and integrity to build commitment and collaboration across organizations and in fractured locales of operation. In the new context, global communication, information transfer and time compression have unleashed a technological tsunami of thought waves, which are reshaping global-local leadership consciousness. This emerging situation is not dis-similar to ocean waves that travel across the globe and wash ashore with great power to reshape the shorescape.

Throughout history, leaders have emerged to respond to crises and shape events. Sometimes in tumultuous times the leader has been able to fabricate understanding of the conditions underlying the crisis and sway people to follow a course of action that has ended in tragedy and disaster. Toxic leaders fail their followers by taking them into a wilderness of destruction and chaos where despair and anguish are the outcomes. Our current leadership context is certainly such a period of dislocation and uncertainty and it is vital to be on guard against leaders who resort to calls to action based on divisiveness, envy, distrust and conflict.

Archetypes, Identity, language and intention – Leadership Capability Stressors

The use of metaphor is vital for visualization and breakthrough thinking. The metaphor of the seven seas illuminates the need for considering emerging leadership approaches in changing contexts. Some of these emerging contexts are geographic others that transfer knowledge and information across nodes of influence to mobilize followers to respond rapidly to situations. Professional archetypes, identity and vested interests of some public, private and NGO institutions make it difficult to collaborate on inter-agency missions in supporting human security, sustainable economic development and human rights. The complexity of inter-connected crisis requires integrative leadership thinking and sense-making frameworks to understand the context, stakeholders, meta-narratives and decision-making required to build the trust and confidence to leverage joint capability in locales of multi-jurisdiction.

The contemporary leadership context is a mind space, not a battle space

Responsible leadership is needed across all segments of society to shape institutions and to create the political, social and economic conditions to improve the wellbeing of people. The challenges of the contemporary context cuts across all communities and all walks of life. The financial order of the world is still recovering from the 2008 Global Financial Crisis which was initiated by the fallout of unscrupulous lending and fake financial derivatives that turned into a global crisis as shockwaves reverberated around the financial system, worsening at each phase until there was a panic around credit. This event was a tipping point that has increased the lack of trust in the financial, government and political arena and resulted in increased polarization of left and right-wing ideologies and self-interest.

The leadership character deficit of the recent past has robbed many of a sense of equity, inclusion, engagement, understanding of history, legacy, community, service and obligation. In the fallout, toxic leaders have been emboldened to pursue a self-serving mindset and hide self-interest and short term thinking behind an overt appeal to addressing crisis to mask an ethical leadership deficit. However, it is fortunate that, despite the leadership deficit, many in this demographic are still positive, motivated and committed to serve and to lead.

Refer to Chapter 3 Leadership Log Self-assessment in understanding resilient character.

Make notes in your log to navigate and lead by example in the contemporary context.

4. Responsible Leadership Confidence – Moral Authority: Trust to Serve and Lead

Too often in the past leadership has been associated with power, greed and hubris. This toxic leadership has and continues to erode trust in leadership and the offices and institutions that it serves. It is time for all hands on to be on deck to respond to the new context. It is time to work the pumps, to rid the toxicity, to navigate and chart a path for responsible leadership if we are to have a future worth living. Fortunately, honesty, hope and good are still alive in the hearts, minds and spirits of those waiting in the sidelines and ready to seize the future to lead onto a better path.

The responsible leader is an individual who inspires a shared vision and inclusive narrative to mobilize a sense of mission and strategic direction to achieve and excel. Responsible leadership is a lofty ambition. However, through courage and determination the everyday reality can be transformed. In the organisational setting leadership is not just about one individual. Instead it is about a shared ethos engendered throughout an organizational culture.

The need to respect human dignity in an era of uncertainty where inter-connected and interdependent crises are challenging leadership in both the developed and developing world. The perpetuation of injustice is no longer just between governments and nation-states. It includes stakeholders who can influence using ideology for both good and bad. Indigenous or community wisdom is often not understood or dis-connected from the sense-making perspective for good governance.

Followership is not necessarily benign – Leadership authority must be earned

Followers can support, influence, agitate, sabotage or desert. In a contemporary context, command and control is shifting to consensus and collaboration. But the nexus between leadership, education and followership is critical. Followers need exemplary leadership role models and wise mentors to help them prepare to potentially lead in a complex contemporary context. This challenge calls for a values shift and an allegiance shift that do not easily respond to old beliefs of tradition, myths, narratives, beliefs and existing mental models of leadership within organizations and communities.

In the West, we are seeing the shift from a relational reciprocal society to a market-driven transactional society. The rise of a transactional culture comes at the cost of a diminution of relationships and a sapping of the sense of obligation required to sustain civic engagement and social contract. In the emerging, developing, fractured world this demographic is awakening linked by social media to witness the daily reality of social, economic, financial, environmental, health and security crises.

To continue to perceive the leader as the head is to ignore the function of the body and corpus of knowledge and interactions that shape and give meaning to context

In leadership it is applied intelligence that breathes life and purpose into the anatomy of the living corporate body of an organization. Yet, the distinct culture of responsible leadership in an organization is hard to develop and replicate. Worldly organizations have sustained leadership and performance largely due to the investment in creating a distinct culture. A culture of responsible leadership is founded on an enlightened ethos, shared vision, core values, mission and strategic direction. A challenge for Western culture is to recognize that self-interest limits cooperation and consensus. Whereas Confucian culture seeks harmony and consensus, this can inhibit individual risk-taking and innovation. As the world becomes more interconnected the intelligent leader learns from both.

Refer to Chapter 4 Leadership Log Self-assessment in understanding confidence.

Make notes in your log to navigate and lead by example in the contemporary context.

5. Responsible Leadership Courage – Uncommon Valor to Lead by example

In the 20th century we have seen how prior generations were called upon to make the ultimate sacrifice and exhibit uncommon valor in times of crisis. However, that shared experience and mind-set is fading in Western society as generations now have known only a relatively stable world order, continued economic prosperity and technological advances for at least the last half-century. Traditional media and social media are more concerned with individual issues of identity, personal values and opinion rather than dealing with discussion around complex issues. Or when complex issues are addressed, there is a tendency to simplify the issue and present it as a tame problem that has uncomplicated solutions. Political leaders are increasingly held hostage to a news media that feeds off social media opinion. The polarised space of social media shuts down discussion and pursues a categorisation of views into a binary of acceptable versus non-acceptable.

Tackling the challenges of the fractured contemporary context will require exceptional, resilient, principled courageous leaders who are schooled not trained in the importance of ethos, morality and character with uncommon mental models for sense-making to make the brave decisions to mobilize and engage followers in hope for the future.

Leadership has deep roots that go back to our ancient ancestors living in groups for security and survival. The leader was and is a trusted beacon of hope for survival.

The emerging voices speak of a need for a new global-local leadership narrative that integrates collective wisdom to sustain people around the world. This type of leadership education has the power to inspire, transform and enlighten new leadership approaches in understanding that crisis and opportunity is part of the same continuum.

Across many communities we see counter-vailing values, ideology, beliefs, identity and intention clash and the result is confusion, conflict, crisis or chaos. Leadership in fractured states is often impacted on by crises imported from another country. This has also mobilized the ideological disenfranchised to export violence as a response.

The global crisis context poses ethical challenges for leadership in organizations. It will require transparency and authenticity to rebuild trust. Leaders have conviction and personal ambitions. They must lead in organizations in contexts where others sometimes disagree. Leadership is required to integrate diverse opinions and political agendas and policy directives in and between organizations. Overall, leadership is about doing the right thing. A leader requires followers. Leadership is a special blend of strategic vision, strategic intent, strategic purpose and strategic direction focused on results.

Refer to Chapter 5 Leadership Log Self-assessment in understanding courage to act.

Make notes in your log to navigate and lead by example in the contemporary context.

6. Responsible Leadership Commitment –Commit and connect for mutual success

In an uncertain and inter-connected world, responsible leadership requires character and moral fortitude to build pathways for peace, hope and reconciliation. Today's crises know no boundaries. Similarly, the power of the leader is transient and changing events and social forces can quickly unseat rulers. The only empires that exist today are empires of the mind. The mental map of the world is fractured and there are many marginalised people on the fringes waiting to be heard.

The new territory presents an opportunity to co-develop a principled ethos founded on harmony for humanity to move forward with a sense of shared purpose and shared vision of healthy community, economic vitality and sustainable development.

Cultivating harmony, hope and opportunity requires the development of the individual's capacity to grow and develop an ethos of responsibility and service. Regrettably, perspectives shaped in the contemporary context tend to accentuate differences not similarities. The prism is often on problems not opportunity. This mindset sustains the status quo and stymies hope and opportunity for millions. In Chinese culture, crisis can be interpreted as representing a continuum that encompasses both danger and opportunity. Leadership can play a pivotal role in shifting the focus onto pathways for equitable human development.

Explore emergent leadership approaches to unleash innovation, hope and success

Leadership development is at a cognitive crossroads. The leadership challenge in the age of super-intelligence is that the leader will need to unlock the mind, body and spirit to leverage new technologies, AI and algorithmic approaches that will shape the future.

It is time to debunk the myth that leader is all-powerful.

This myth can get in the way of worthwhile change since it fosters mindsets and ways of seeing and doing that ignore the need for leaders to continually reflect on their limitations and to overcome them. Leaders without self-awareness and insight into their own limitations contribute to the conflict and problems that underpin confusion and conflict.

The dominant management school and "leadership industry" approach to learning has focused on the idea of the individual agency of the organizational leader as received wisdom in the face of disconfirming evidence. It's time we removed that narrative. The popular folklore of leadership links organizational success or failure directly to the actions of a powerful leader. The context today requires a responsible leadership mindset, ethos and decision-making to transform and leverage leadership capacity in education, public service and business organizations.

Refer to Chapter 6 Leadership Log Self-assessment in understanding shared commitment.

Make notes in your log to navigate and lead by example in the contemporary context.

7. Responsible Leadership Capability – ROI2 Return on Intelligence and Integrity

The challenges of the contemporary context cut across all countries and all walks of life.

The world is both nationalistic and a global village made up of diverse tribes that are digitally interconnected and aware, where shocks are transmitted at cyber speed. Leadership is often impacted on by crisis imported from another country. This percolation of dislocation often mobilizes the ideological disenfranchised to export violence as response.

The emerging voices of hope speak of a need for a new leadership narrative that integrates collective wisdom to sustain people and communities. This type of leadership has the power to inspire, transform and enlighten new approaches in understanding that crisis and opportunity are part of the same continuum.

The seven principles 7C of leadership, the leader is seen as captain, navigator and explorer to take followers to new heights of purpose and performance.

The leadership challenge calls for an informed perspective to cultivate the meaning, understanding and expression of "leader agency" as a shared belief that is socially constructed to recognize that leaders are co-participants in the social construction of meaning and purpose. This change in thinking will heighten follower efforts in achieving worthy outcomes to serve and lead.

Challenge popular leadership myths and methods

To achieve this goal, the authors mentored responsible leadership development with many career professionals of diverse beliefs, ethnicity and gender to serve and lead in diverse and at times dangerous contexts have used the lessons learned from Shackleton's leadership story. There are some important implications to consider here. Primarily, Shackleton exhibited leadership within a self-sufficient community without the support and backing of an authority structure that had the power to sanction or reward followers.

Shackleton did not try to beat nature or to conquer the Antarctic. Instead Shackleton displayed a positive and responsible relationship-based style of leadership that enabled the group to maintain itself in a crisis and to pursue a clear plan of action that resulted in a valued objective, which for the expedition was returning home safely.

Refer to Chapter 7 Leadership Log Self-assessment in understanding resilient capability.

Make notes in your log to navigate and lead by example in the contemporary context.

Chapter Summary

The need for collaborative leadership-followership in the contemporary context

This collaborative leadership style works well within contemporary organizational and social contexts where all employees, irrespective of gender or race, are self-motivated and where diversity provides the competitive advantage.

The scientific research indicates that relationship-based leadership styles are very effective. Today, professions, institutions and agencies increasingly will be required to collaborate in integrated approaches to respond to complex situations.

This collaborative approach requires a leadership ethos that values humility, empathy, trust, transparency, accountability and dialogue. At the same time, it must have strength of character and conviction to stand against deceit, duplicity, silent sabotage and threat. This leadership ethos is founded on the wisdom exhibited by exemplary leaders.

The principled leader is bound by a code of conduct, service and sacrifice. Working within a culture of leadership, they have the existential power to mobilize people and sustain communities.

Leadership is a dynamic activity that comes alive as the leader works with followers to achieve worthy outcomes. This definition is at odds with views that leadership is an inherent quality to be found within the leader or that leadership is a generic pursuit that can be understood without reference to context or a historical time and place. Our definition of leadership challenges the assumed understanding of leadership taught in many business schools - that leadership can be reduced to set of generic characteristics or behaviors.

Instead, leadership, as a dynamic activity, depends on the capacity of the leader to relate to people in shifting social contexts and influence people to pursue worthy outcomes. The self-mastery of this mindset provides new insights to foster trust, integrity and measure the hidden costs of what matters.

Each of the principles explored are essential to cultivate the leadership mindset to be a responsible principled leader. It is a life-long pursuit. It requires heart, mind and spirit to engender a serving ethos in life and work. It is the ability that energizes words, deeds and acts for positive change to unleash the human potential for good works.

Shackleton's responsible leadership is required today to meet the leadership challenge in a fluid context and unknown future horizon.

A call to action is needed to respond to the worldwide context where leaders need to develop their own capacity for responsible leadership.

It is time to navigate the 7Cs and explore a path worth living founded on hope, and opportunity for those we serve and lead as a legacy for the future.

You are now ready to step on the ice and become the principled leader, champion, navigator and agent of change that leads with principles and purpose to serve, lead and excel and create a better future in life, work and community.

This is a noble and worthy legacy of the principled leader comprised in considered thoughts, worthy principles, motivating words, ethical deeds and responsible action.

Responsible Leadership Log - Action Planning

In reading the book you are ready to implement responsible principled leadership in action. The Seven Seas 7Cs responsible leadership principles framework is designed for individual development and high potential teams in your organization. At the end of each chapter reflect on key lessons learned and teachable moments. Note these in your Leadership Log as a source of reference as you master the art of responsible leadership in action. Start to identify potential gaps in your leadership. Be sure to recognize those opportunities when you excel in a specific context and also when you have to deal with adverse and crisis scenarios. Applying the 7Cs can benefit you as a leader at work, home and in other endeavors. Like Shackleton's voyage it is a resilience-building journey. Take time for personal renewal to sustain you in the applied learning process. Be sure to celebrate milestones and achievement. The end goal is living a legacy of responsible principled leadership. Mentoring others in responsible leadership is a worthy object to enable others to excel.

1. Dedicate time to reflect on important lessons learned in each chapter

2. Make notes in your log as you proceed through the seven principles.
This includes:
- Lessons learned.
- Notes to self for review.
- Specific goals and objectives to strengthen leadership.
- Observations from daily work or news examples of responsible leadership

3. As you start this leadership journey take a bearing on where you are now and where you want to be in a specific timeline. This includes:
- Know Thyself – How do you rate as a leader at this point?

What do you need to work on to serve, lead and excel as a responsible leader?
- Be honest and recognize that as a leader we are all human and a work in progress.

4. Ethos, Pathos, Logos
Review the readings on ethos, pathos, and logos.
- Note how well you are developing all three spheres to strengthen your leadership capability and personal resilience.

5. What is your personal mission as a responsible leader?
- Develop your own vision and mission statements to sustain goals and objectives.
- Reflect on the key personal values that underpin your leadership character.

6. What is your unique or distinct leadership capability?
- What does it say about you as a leader?
- How does it manifest in good words, works and deeds.

7. Navigating the Seven Seas in a time of change, crisis and disruption.
- What makes you an authentic leader in serving and leading others?
- What does your leadership narrative say to leverage your

General References and Selected Bibliography

Admiralty, Manual of Seamanship: Volume 1. His Majesty's Stationary Office, London, 1937.

Aldersey-Williams, H. The Tide: The Science and Stories Behind the Greatest Force on Earth. W. W. Norton & Company, New York, 2016.

Amundsen, R. Roald Amundsen: A Biography. Sutton Publishing Ltd., Stroud., 2006.

Baker, K. Mutiny, Terrorism, Riots and Murder: A History of Sedition in Australia and New Zealand. Rosenburg, Australia. 2006.

Barrie, D. Sextant.. William Morrow, New York, 2014.

Brandt, A. The Tragic History of the Sea: Shipwrecks from the Bible to Titanic. National Geographic, Washington, 2006.

Chichester, F. The Lonely Sea and The Sky. Pan Books Ltd. London, 1967.

Davis W., Into The Silence: The Great War, Mallory, and the Conquest of Everest. Alfred A. Knopf, New York, 2011.

Dunlop, G. D. & Shufeldt, H. H. Dutton's, Navigation and Piloting. Naval Institute Press, Annapolis, 1972.

Elder, J. Walking - Henry David Thoreau. Beacon Press, Boston, 1991.

Fiennes, R. Mind over Matter: The Epic Crossing of The Antarctic Continent. Sinclair-Stevenson, London, 1993.

Flemin, F. Barrow's Boys: The Original Extreme Adventure. Atlantic Monthly Press, New York, 1998.

Freedman, L. Strategy: A History. Oxford University Press, New York, 2013.

Gardner, H. in collaboration with Laskin, E. Leading Minds An Anatomy of Leadership. Perseus Books Group, New York, 1996.

Frankl, V. E. Man's Search for Meaning. Washington Square Press, New York, 1985.

Grint, K. Leadership: Limits and Possibilities. Palgrave Macmillan, New York, 2005.

Heacox, K. Shackleton: The Antarctic Challenge. National Geographic, Washington, D.C.

Heyerdahl, T. The Ra Expeditions, New American Library, New York, 1972.

Hoare, P. The Whale: In Search of the Giants of the Sea. Ecco Imprint by Harper Collins, New York ,2010.,

Hunter, D. Against The Odds: The Incredible Story of *Evergreen* and the Canada's Cup. Personal Library, Publishers, Toronto, 1981.

Humphreys, W., Mackie, P. & W., Bacon. A. Global Challenge: Leadership Lessons from the World's Toughest Yacht Race, The Book Guild, Ltd. Lewes, Sussex, 1998.

Hurley, F. South With Endurance, Shackleton's Antarctic Expedition 1914-1917 The Photographs of Frank Hurley. BCL Press, New York, 2004.

Husick, C. B. Chapman Piloting & Seamanship, Hearst Books, New York, 2009.

Johnson, W. B. & Harper, G. P. Becoming a Leader: The Annapolis Way. McGraw-Hill, New York, 2005.

Jones, M. Editor: Robert Falcon Scott Journals Captain Scott's Last Expedition. Oxford University Press, Oxford, 2005.

Kellerman, B. Leadership: Multidisciplinary Perspectives. Prentice-Hall, New Jersey, 1984.

Kempster, S. How Managers Have Learnt to Lead: Exploring the Development of Leadership Practice. Palgrave Macmillan, New York, 2009.

Knox-Johnston. R. Force of Nature. Penguin Books, London, 2007.

Lansing, A. Endurance:: Shackleton's Incredible Voyage. Carol & Graf Publishers, New York, 1959.

Legace-Roy, D. & Krackstedt, J. Mentoring Handbook. The Canadian Forces Leadership Institute, Ottawa, 2007.

Lowe G. & Lewis-Jones, H. The Crossing of Antarctica. Thames Hudson Ltd., London, 2014.

Mawson, D. The Home of the Blizzard: A Heroic Tale of Antarctic Exploration and Survival. Skyhorse, Unabridged edition, 2013.

Mayers, A. Beyond Endurance: 300 Boats, 600 Miles, And One Deadly Sea. McClelland & Stewart, Toronto, 2007.

Morrell. M. & Capparell, S. Shackleton's Way. Viking, New York, 2001.

Owen, R. The Conquest of the North and South Poles: Adventures of the Peary and Byrd Expeditions. Random House, New York, 1952.

Palin, M. Erebus: One Ship, Two Epic Voyages, and the Greatest Naval Mystery of all Time. Random House Canada,, 2018.

Penny, H. L One Hundred Years and Still Sailing, D. G. Selden Printing Co. Ltd., Hamilton, 1988.

Robertson, D. Sea Survival: A Manual. Praeger Publishers, New York, 1975.

Shackleton E. Escape from the Antarctic, taken from South: The Endurance Expedition. Penguin Books, London, first published 1909.

Shriberg, A., Lloyd C., Shriberg, D., Williamson, M.N. Practicing Leadership: Principles and Applications. John Wiley & Sons Inc. New York, 1997.

Slocum: Sailing Alone Around the World.. Penguin Books, New York. 1999.

Smalley, D. Poems of Robert Browning. Houghton Mifflin Company, Boston, 1956.

Sobel, D. Longitude: The True Story of a Lone Genius Who Solved the Greatest Scientific Problems of His Time. Bloomsbury, USA, 2007.

Sobel, D. Galileo's Daughter: A Historical Memoir of Science, Faith and Love. Bloomsbury, New York, 2011.

Smiles, S. Duty: Courage, Patience and Endurance. A. L. Burt Company, New York, 1919.

Spufford, F. The Antarctic: An Anthology. Granta Publications, London, 2007.

Tennyson, A. Poetical Works of Alfred Lord Tennyson. Macmillan & Co. Ltd, New York, 1899.

Turnball, S., Case P., Edwards, G., Schedlitzki., D. Simpson., P. Simpson. Worldly Leadership: Alternative Wisdoms for a Complex World. Palgrave Macmillan, New York, 2012.

Turney, C. 1912 The Year the World Discovered Antarctica. Counterpoint, Berkeley, 2012.

Williams, G. The Quest for the Northwest Passage. Folio Society, London. 2014.

Winchester, S. Atlantic: Great Sea battles, Heroic Discoveries, Titanic Storms and a Vast Ocean of a Million Stories. Harper Collins, New York, 201.

Winchester, S. Pacific: Silicon Chips and Surfboards, Coral Reefs and Atom Bombs, Brutal Dictators, Fading Empires, and the Coming Collision of the World's Superpowers. Harper Collins Canada, Toronto, 2015.

Wiseman, J. SAS Survival Guide. Harper Collins, Glasgow. 1993.

Worsley, F. A. Shackleton's Boat Journey. W. W. Norton & Company, Inc. New York, 1977.

Authors' Relevant Publications and Conference Papers

Warn, J. "Strategic Leadership in an Era of Complexity and Uncertainty". In International Perspectives on Military Leadership (eds) Douglas Lindsay, Daniel Watola, & Dave Woycheshin. Ottawa: Director General Military Personnel Research and Analysis. 2018. Ch 12 pp 217- 234.

Stewart J, Warn J. Between two worlds: Indigenous leaders exercising influence and working across boundaries. Australian Journal of Public Administration. 2017; 76(1):3-17.

Cox, M. & Warn. J., "The Leader is Leadership." In Organizational Processes and Received Wisdom, IAP Publishing, Edited by D. J. Svyantek and K. T. Mahoney, 2014. Ch 2 pp 29 - 48. ISBN 978-1-62396-550-1.

Okros. A., Cox, M., Warn. J. "The Intellectual Challenges of Complexity in Contemporary Military Missions." In Leadership in Challenging Situations, Peter Lang Publishing, Frankfurt, 2012. Ch 1 p23 - 65. ISBN 978-3-631-62273-5.

Dhalla R., Cox, M., Magee C, Warn J. International Panel and Workshop on Research and Education of Leadership and Corporate Social Responsibility in Messy Contexts. Academy of Management's East meets West Annual Conference, San Antonio, Texas, 2011.

Van Duren E. & Cox, M. Responsible Leadership and Strategic Management. Custom text and Casebook on Business Strategy. ISBN-13: 978-0-558-77463-9 Published by Pearson, 2010.

Warn, J. & Cox, M. Leadership as Sense-Making for Capacity Building. Paper submitted for the International Congress of Applied Psychology, Melbourne, Australia, 2010.

Cox, M. & Magee, C. Collaborative Leadership and Coalition-Building in Crisis Contexts. Paper Presentation. Inter-University Seminar on Armed Forces and Society, Conference, Toronto, 2010.

Warn. J. & Cox, M. Leadership across Boundaries for Peace and Security: A Canadian Perspective, FRP Report, Department of

Foreign Affairs and International Trade. Government of Canada, 2010.

Cox, M. Leadership in Crisis, Keynote Address, Annual Seminar, Department of Finance, Government of Canada, Ottawa, 2009.

Cox, M., Hess, M., Okros, A., Warn, J. Towards 3D+C "Whole of Government Leadership", Leadership Seminar Presentation, Canadian School of Public Service, Ottawa, 2009.

Cox M. &Warn J. Educating Future Leaders in Sense-Making and Decision-Making in Complex Contexts and Locales to Secure, Build, Sustain Leadership, Culture and Capability, International Conference Paper, Studying Leadership Conference, University of Auckland, 2008.

Cox, M., Strategic Leadership for Collaboration and Cooperation in Aligning Security, Trade Development and Human Rights in an Era of Uncertainty. Conference presentation, Oxford University, 2008.

Cox, M. A Values-Based Leadership Framework: Ethics and Accountability, Panel paper, Public Sector Leadership in the 21st Century, International Leadership Conference, Centre for Studies in Leadership, University of Guelph, 2007.

International Leadership Applied Field Research

The following is a list of institutions the author's have engaged with in applied leadership research that helped inform the book.

Auckland University, Leadership Conference.

Australian Defense Force Academy, Leadership Program.

Australian Federal Police Academy, Field Research.

Bristol University, Studying Leadership Conference.

China Executive Leadership Academy, Pudong, Shanghai.

Canadian School for Public Service.

Canadian International Development Agency.

Canadian Police Academy.

Canadian Forces Leadership Academy.

Cranfield University, Leadership Conference.

Defence Research Academy, Canada.

Hamilton General Hospital.

Hamilton Health Sciences.

International Leadership Association, Washington.

Institute for Public Administration, Canada.

Inter-University Seminar on Armed Forces and Society, Chicago.

International Military Testing Association.

Marriott Corporation.

Ministry of Finance Canada.

Ontario Police College.

Peel Region Police.

Oxford Round Table on Leadership and Security.

Royal Military College of Canada.

Royal Hamilton Yacht Club.

Seneca College of Applied Arts & Technology.

Toronto Police Service.

Toronto Police Training Academy.

University of Guelph, Leadership Advisory Board.

University of New South Wales, Visiting Fellow Research.

Warwick University, IGPM Leadership Conference.

York Region Police.

Author's Profile

Dr. Michael Cox is Professor Emeritus in Leadership at the University of Guelph. He has served as Graduate Faculty and Director, Centre for Studies in Leadership.

He works with career professionals in leadership development in the serving professions. He was a Visiting Fellow in Leadership at UNSW at the Australian Defence Force Academy. Michael worked with the co-author for over a decade on comparative international research on leadership in complex contexts with health, police, defence and the serving professions. Michael is graduate faculty at the Gordon S. Lang School of Business and Economics, University of Guelph and advisory board member on Leadership Programs. He is a Fellow of the Royal Society of Arts. He served as a naval officer on operations in the Canadian Forces and as a unit information officer, Director General information branch and National Headquarters. He is Past Commodore of a sail-training club and an exhibited marine artist. He has worked on projects to address leadership, ethos, change and capability in government, academic and private sector organizations. **He can be contacted at: drmcoxfaculty@gmail.com or Linkedin.**

Dr. James Warn is Former Head, School of Business and Leadership Programs, Australian Defence Force Academy at the University of New South Wales.

He works with career professionals in defence and the serving professions. He was a Visiting Scholar in Leadership at the University of Guelph and worked with the co-author of the book for over a decade in comparative international research on leadership development in complex context with defence, police and the serving professions. James is a registered psychologist, a member Australian Psychological Society, a Fellow of the College of Organisational Psychologists, and a former Committee Member for the Sydney Branch Australian Psychological Society, and former Chair of the ACT section of the College of Organisational Psychologists. He has served as an officer in the Australian Army and was a unit commander and during his postings to military headquarters he worked on major organisational change projects. He has worked on projects addressing organisational change and has published on leadership and immigrant entrepreneurship. **He can be contacted at:** warnjrw@gmail.com **or Linkedin.**

www.ingramcontent.com/pod-product-compliance
Lightning Source LLC
Chambersburg PA
CBHW071540220526
45469CB00003B/861